RIDING LOW
on the STREETS of
GOLD

Edited, with an Introduction, by

Judith Ortiz Cofer

PIÑATA BOOKS
ARTE PÚBLICO PRESS
HOUSTON, TEXAS

This volume is made possible through grants from the National Endowment for the Arts and the City of Houston through The Cultural Arts Council of Houston, Harris County.

Piñata Books are full of surprises!

Piñata Books
An imprint of Arte Público Press
University of Houston
452 Cullen Performance Hall
Houston, Texas 77204-2004

Cover illustration and design by Lamberto Alvarez
Initial anthology selections by Georgina Baeza and Karina Hernández

Ortiz Cofer, Judith.
    Riding Low on the Streets of Gold: Latino literature for young adults / edited, with an introduction by Judith Ortiz Cofer.
        p.   cm.
    Contents: I / José Martí—Amanda / Roberta Fernández—sel. from ...*y no se lo tragó la tierra,* The Salamanders / Tomás Rivera—The Fabulous Sinkhole / Jesús Salvador Treviño—Fences, Same Song, Tomás Rivera / Pat Mora—Growing / Helena María Viramontes—Haunt, Walking Home / Sarah Cortez—Carrying Sergei / Mike Padilla—He Couldn't Guess My Name / Jesús Colón—Pillars of Gold and Silver / Beatriz de la Garza—Religious Instructions for Young Casualties, Affirmations #3, Take Off Your Mask, Life Is A Journey / Sandra María Esteves—Ricardito / Virgil Suárez—Too White / Daniel Chacón—*Toreando el tren* or Bullfighting the Train / Victor Villaseñor—Primary Lessons, Volar / Judith Ortiz Cofer.
    ISBN 1-55885-380-4 (alk. paper).
    1. Hispanic Americans—Literary collections. 2. American literature—Hispanic authors. [1. Hispanic Americans—Literary collections. 2. American literature—Hispanic American authors—Collections.]
    I. Ortiz Cofer, Judith, 1952-
    PZ5+860.8′09283′089068073—dc22
                                                                    2003061231
                                                                        CIP
⊗ The paper used in this publication meets the requirements of the American National Standard for Information Sciences—Permanence of Paper for Printed Library Materials, ANSI Z39.48-1984.

Introduction © 2003 by Judith Ortiz Cofer
Printed in the United States of America

3 4 5 6 7 8 9 0 1 2   10 9 8 7 6 5 4 3 2 1

Contents

Judith Ortiz Cofer
Introduction   v

José Martí
I   2

Roberta Fernández
Amanda   9

Tomás Rivera
from ...*y no se lo tragó la tierra* / ...*And the Earth Did Not
    Devour Him* 23
The Salamanders 24

Jesús Salvador Treviño
The Fabulous Sinkhole 30

Pat Mora
Fences 61
Same Song 62
Tomás Rivera 63

Helena María Viramontes
Growing 66

Sarah Cortez

Haunt 78

Walking Home 79

Mike Padilla

Carrying Sergei 81

Jesús Colón

He Couldn't Guess My Name 119

Beatriz de la Garza

Pillars of Gold and Silver 122

Sandra María Esteves

Religious Instructions for Young Casualties 140

Affirmations #3, Take Off Your Mask 142

Life Is A Journey 142

Virgil Suárez

Ricardito 144

Daniel Chacón

Too White 147

Victor Villaseñor

· *Toreando el tren* or Bullfighting the Train 166

Judith Ortiz Cofer

Primary Lessons 186

Volar 194

Additional Works by These Authors 197

Introduction

We are shaped by the stories we hear and read during our lives. Our personal narratives elevate us beyond the daily struggle for survival, giving our *luchas* meaning and purpose. *Las luchas* over the little and big hurdles we must conquer and the battles we must win in order to become strong and free individuals, have to be preserved as *cuentos y poemas* so that others will learn from our victories as well as from our mistakes and failures. We must share the *cuentos*, these stories that taught us how to be human, not just how to be male/female or nonwhite/white. The stories don't even have to have actually happened to anyone in particular or even in the real world, but they have to be *la verdad*—true as all good stories are true, true because we believe them and because we identify with the characters and situations in them.

In *Riding Low on the Streets of Gold: Latino Literature for Young Adults,* most of the stories and poems are told in the voices of young people undergoing the passages that are common to all human beings in the process of becoming mature adults: the parental conflicts, the sibling rivalries, the comings of age, the excitement of first loves, and the grief of loss. In them we find good and bad characters, angry and even violent people, as well as saintly ones. We meet barrio witches, cursing and spitting grandmothers, saintly *abuelitas* and kind strangers. Yet what differentiates this collection from others of its kind is its focus on the special skills that young people of Latino heritage—those of us who are marked by language, ethnicity, economic and social factors as *los otros*, the outsiders—must master in order to join the bigger circle of American mainstream society. In some cases, the circle will not allow another pair of hands to join in—and there is a lesson in this, too. Perhaps it was not *that* circle that mattered, perhaps it was something greater than social acceptance that was at stake: family loyalties or the need to be recognized as an individual instead of as simply part of the group. The key almost always seems to lie in communication, in making the effort to break through the silences.

One of the main topics of my own writing of stories and poems as a bicultural American is how language can be used as a tool, a weapon, and best of all for me, as material for art. I am constantly fascinated by the power words have to enhance and to enrich our lives—and in some cases also to hurt us.

Through sharing the experiences of those who came before us, the writers of *Riding Low on the Streets of Gold: Latino Literature for Young Adults* take the readers along on their journeys. Some of these *viajes* are joyous celebrations of culture and family; others are angry protests at the pain people inflict on one another simply because of misconceptions and prejudices (in some cases the tables are turned and peer pressure forces the brown teenager to betray his white friend in order to save face). In each of the pieces, however, we find an authentic human voice speaking in an accent the reader will recognize as familiar, guiding us down a path of knowledge through shared experiences. We hold our heads high as we go *Riding Low on the Streets of Gold.*

These stories and poems are also about breaking through the wall of silence that we construct around us as protection when we feel alone and alienated. It is a wall that must be brought down before we can become fully at home with others and, consequently, with ourselves.

Many years ago when I arrived in this country as a Spanish-speaking immigrant child, I approached English in fear but with excitement and hope. I knew even then that not until I both fully possessed the language of *mi familia*, Spanish, and gained power over the language of my future survival, English, would I have a homeland. I would be confined to the small space between languages and cultures; I would always feel left out, marginalized. In my languages, I have found my homeland. It is a bicultural, bilingual place, and I am completely at home here where I can enjoy everything twice over.

I define *my* homeland as the imaginary place from which my creative energy arises. It is not necessarily a geographic location, but rather a state of being that fills me with a sense of belonging. Now that I have written a few books, I am discovering a pattern in my work: all of my years in America, I have been weaving my life into the tapestry of American history, I have been blending the language of my origin, my dreams, and my imagination, Spanish, with the language of my new life, English, in order create a new way of being an American. Doesn't that make the world more interesting? To be able to hear and understand in both Spanish and English, to have a choice in the language of our dreams?

And isn't that what we all do in our own ways in our own words, that is, blending our story to the story of our times? Whether set in the time of the Mexican or Cuban Revolutions, or the beginning of the big Puerto Rican migration to this country, the writers in this collection are talking about you and me, telling the stories of every one of us who has felt isolated by language, skin color, or anything else that did not fit the big picture. We, the Latinos and Latinas in the United States, have learned to find ways to add our stories to the story of the new place. Now we must learn to feel privileged to have two languages and two cultures to draw from and to celebrate.

Although I see myself as a Spanish-speaking Latina, I also understand that I live my working life in English, and I feel a sense of pride in claiming to have two cultures that are like concentric circles within which I find my comfort zone. I have also redefined the word *home* to mean the place where I am a part of the story being created. It is a flexible definition, another tool of survival in a world where our real homeland may exist in our imaginations, in our dreams, and in the memories our *antepasados* left us as an inheritance that belongs to us only in our time, that we have a choice to neglect or to preserve and pass down to the next generation. Our cultural homeland will exist only for as long as we love it and practice it: the traditions, poems, stories, customs, rites, music, songs—thus, it is a homeland you may take with you or recycle to make it your own, a homeland that is fully yours, as it should be. The stories contained in this anthology are a feast of words and ideas.

They are a portable fiesta you can set up anywhere you wish to go. These are the stories that belong to you and to me: the shared homeland of our Latino/a cultures. And that is what I mean by *Riding Low on the Streets of Gold.*

Judith Ortiz Cofer
Athens, Georgia
June 30, 2003

José Martí

Born in Havana, Cuba, on January 28, 1853, José Martí began his political and literary careers at the early age of fifteen, when he helped found a Havana newspaper opposing colonialism. At seventeen, his radical politics drove him into exile in Spain, where he established himself as a poet and a playwright. Martí returned to the Americas with a degree in law and in 1875 settled in Mexico, where his literary career flourished. In 1878, Martí went back to Cuba, but a year later his conspiracy against Spanish authorities banished him to Spain once again. Martí soon left Spain to go to New York, where he stayed for a year, and then went to Venezuela. He returned to New York in 1881, after being forced to leave Venezuela by its dictatorial leadership. In New York, Martí was appointed to several diplomatic positions and published *Ismaelillo* (1882), *La edad de oro* (1889), *Patria* (1890–1895, Key West). He also wrote for *La Nación*, a Buenos Aires newspaper. In 1891, Martí published his collection of poetry, *Versos Sencillos*, portraying his life in a country that enjoyed both liberty and freedom, expressing a yearning for that liberty in his own country. In 1895, Martí returned to his native country to fight in the war for Cuban independence, and it was there, on May 19, that he died a national hero. As a politician, José Martí founded a revolutionary party that in 1889 liberated Cuba. As a poet, he started a revolutionary movement in literature, the Modernist movement, securing Martí's place as one of the greatest poets of his time.

I

Yo soy un hombre sincero
de donde crece la palma,
y antes de morirme quiero
echar mis versos del alma.

Yo vengo de todas partes,
y hacia todas partes voy:
Arte soy entre las artes,
en los montes, monte soy.

Yo sé los nombres extraños
de las yerbas y las flores,
y de mortales engaños,
y de sublimes dolores.

Yo he visto en la noche oscura
llover sobre mi cabeza
los rayos de lumbre pura
de la divina belleza.

Alas nacer vi en los hombros
de las mujeres hermosas:
Y salir de los escombros
volando las mariposas.

He visto vivir a un hombre
con el puñal al costado,
sin decir jamás el nombre
de aquella que lo ha matado.

I

A sincere man am I
from the land where palm trees grow,
and I want before I die
my soul's verses to bestow.

I'm a traveler to all parts,
and a newcomer to none;
I am art among the arts,
with the mountains I am one.

I know the strange names of willows,
and can tell flowers with skill:
I know of lies that can kill,
and I know of sublime sorrows.

I have seen through dead of night
upon my head softly fall,
rays formed of the purest light
from beauty celestial.

I have seen wings that were surging
from beautiful women's shoulders,
and seen butterflies emerging
from the refuse heap that moulders.

I have known a man to live
with a dagger at his side,
and never once the name give
of she by whose hand he died.

Yo sé bien que cuando el mundo
cede, lívido, al descanso,
sobre el silencio profundo
murmura el arroyo manso.

Yo he puesto la mano osada,
de horror y júbilo yerta,
sobre la estrella apagada
que cayó frente a mi puerta.

Oculto en mi pecho bravo
la pena que me lo hiere:
El hijo de un pueblo esclavo
vive por él, calla, y muere.

Todo es hermoso y constante,
todo es música y razón,
y todo, como el diamante,
antes que luz es carbón.

Yo sé que el necio se entierra
con gran lujo y con gran llanto,—
y que no hay fruta en la tierra
como la del camposanto.

Callo, y entiendo, y me quito
la pompa del rimador:
Cuelgo de un árbol marchito
mi muceta de doctor.

I know that the world is weak
and must soon fall to the ground,
and, then, midst the quiet profound
the gentle brook will speak.

While trembling with joy and dread,
I have touched with hand so bold
a once-bright star that fell dead
from heaven at my threshold.

I have hid in my brave heart
the most terrible of pains,
the son of a land in chains
lives for it and dies apart.

All is beautiful and right,
all is as music and reason;
and as diamonds ere their season,
all is coal before its light.

I know when fools are laid to rest
honor and tears will abound,
and that of all fruits, the best
is left to rot in holy ground.

Without a word, I've understood
and put aside the pompous muse;
from a withered branch, I choose
to hang my doctoral hood.

Rápida, como un reflejo,
dos veces vi el alma, dos:
Cuando murió el pobre viejo,
cuando ella me dijo adiós.

Temblé una vez,—en la reja,
a la entrada de la viña,—
cuando la bárbara abeja
picó en la frente a mi niña.

Gocé una vez, de tal suerte
que gocé cual nunca:—cuando
la sentencia de mi muerte
leyó el alcaide llorando.

Oigo un suspiro, a través
de las tierras y la mar,
y no es un suspiro,—es
que mi hijo va a despertar.

Si dicen que del joyero
tome la joya mejor,
tomo a un amigo sincero
y pongo a un lado el amor.

Yo he visto al águila herida
volar al azul sereno,
y morir en su guarida
la víbora del veneno.

Twice, for an instant, did I
my soul's reflection descried,
twice: when my poor father died,
and when she bade me good-bye.

I trembled once, when I flung
the vineyard gate, and to my dread,
the dastard hornet had stung
my little girl on the forehead.

Such great luck to me once came
as no man would dare to envy,
when in tears my jailer read me
the death warrant with my name.

I hear a sigh across the earth,
I hear a sigh over the deep:
It is no sigh reaching my hearth,
but my son waking from sleep.

If they say I have obtained
the pick of the jeweller's trove,
a good friend is all I've gained,
and I have put aside love.

I have seen an eagle gliding,
though wounded, across the skies;
I know the cubby where lies
the snake of its venom dying.

Roberta Fernández

Born and raised near the Texas-Mexico border in Laredo, Texas, Roberta Fernández grew up listening to her mother tell stories of the mixed border culture. Spending most of her adult life in California, Fernández earned a Ph.D. in Romance Languages and Literature from the University of California at Berkeley in 1990, with a specialization in Latin-American literature. In her writing, Fernández portrays women who, living in a patriarchal society, were not allowed to voice their feelings and opinions. Her work acknowledges how Latin-American women have influenced their communities and how valuable they are and have been to Latino culture, especially to more recent generations. Among her published work, Fernández has written *Intaglio: A Novel in Six Stories* (1990) and the Spanish version of *Intaglio*, entitled *Fronterizas: Una novela en seis cuentos* (2001). She is also editor of *In Other Words: Literature by Latinas of the United States* (1994). Fernández's *Intaglio* won the 1991 Best Fiction award from Multicultural Publishers Exchange. Fernández is currently an assistant professor at the University of Georgia, Atlanta, in the Department of Romance Languages and Women's Studies.

Amanda

¿Dónde está el niño que yo fui,
sigue dentro de mí o se fue?

❦ ❦ ❦

¿Por qué anduvimos tanto tiempo
creciendo para separarnos?

Pablo Neruda

I

Transformation was definitely her specialty, and out of georgettes, piques, peaux de soie, organzas, shantungs, and laces, she made exquisite gowns adorned with delicate opaline beadwork, which she carefully touched up with the thinnest slivers of iridescent cording that one could find. At that time I was so captivated by Amanda's creations that often before I fell asleep, I would conjure up visions of her workroom, where luminous whirls of *lentejuelas de concha nácar* would be dancing about, softly brushing against the swaying fabrics in various shapes and stages of completion. Then, amidst the colorful threads and iridescent fabrics shimmering in a reassuring rhythm, she would get smaller and smaller until she was only the tiniest of gray dots among the colors and lights, and slowly, slowly, the uninterrupted gentle droning of the magical Singer sewing machine and her mocking, whispering voice would both vanish into a silent, solid darkness.

By day, whenever I had the opportunity, I loved to sit next to her machine, observing her hands guiding the movement of the fabrics. I was so moved by what I saw that she soon grew to intimidate me and I almost never originated conversation. Therefore, our only communication for long stretches of time was my obvious fascination with the changes that transpired before my watchful eyes. Finally she would look up at me through her gold-rimmed glasses and ask *"¿Te gusta, muchacha?"*

In response to my nod she would proceed to tell me familiar details about the women who would be showing off her finished costumes at the Black and White Ball or at some other such event.

Rambling on with the reassurance of someone who has given considerable thought to everything she says, Amanda would then mesmerize me even further with her provocative gossip about the men and women who had come to our area many years before. Then, as she tied a thread here and added a touch there, I would feel compelled to ask her a question or two as my flimsy contribution to our lengthy conversation.

With most people I chatted freely, but with Amanda I seldom talked since I had the distinct feeling by the time I was five or six that, in addition to other apprehensions I had about her, she felt total indifference towards me. "How can she be so inquisitive?" I was positive she would be saying to herself even as I persisted with another question.

When she stopped talking to concentrate fully on what she was doing, I would gaze directly at her, admiring how beautiful she looked. Waves of defeat would overtake me, for the self-containment that she projected behind her austere appearance made me think she would never take notice of me, while I loved everything about her. I would follow the shape of her head from the central part of her dark auburn hair pulled down over her ears to the curves of the bun she wore at the nape of her long neck. Day in and day out she wore a gray shirtwaist with a narrow skirt and elbow-length sleeves, which made her seem even taller than she was. The front had tiny stitched-down vertical pleats and a narrow deep pocket in which she sometimes tucked her eyeglasses. A row of straight pins with big plastic heads ran down the front of her neckline, and a yellow measuring tape hung around her neck. Like the rest of the relatives, she seemed reassuringly permanent in the uniform she had created for herself.

Her day lasted from seven in the morning until nine in the evening. During this time she could dash off in a matter of two or three days an elaborate wedding dress or a classically simple evening gown for someone's fifteen-year-old party, and Veronica would then embroider the garment. Her disposition did not require her to concentrate on any one outfit from start to finish, and this allowed her to work on many at once. It also meant she had dresses everywhere, hanging from the edge of the doors, on a wall-to-wall bar suspended near the ceiling, and on three or four tables where they would be carefully laid out.

Once or twice, she managed to make a hysterical bride late to her own wedding. In those hectic instances, Amanda would have the sobbing bride step inside her dress, then hold her breath while she sewed in the back zipper by hand. Somehow people did not seem to mind these occasional slip-ups, for they kept coming back, again and again, from Saltillo and Monterrey, from San Antonio and Corpus Christi, and a few even from far-off Dallas and Houston. Those mid-Texas socialites seemed to enjoy practicing their very singular Spanish with Amanda, who never once let on that she really did speak perfect English, and, only after they were gone, would she chuckle over her little joke with us.

As far as her other designs went, her initial basic dress pattern might be a direct copy from *Vogue* magazine, or it could stem from someone's wildest fantasy. From then on, the creation was Amanda's, and every one of her clients trusted the final look to her own discretion. The svelte Club Campestre set from Monterrey and Nuevo Laredo would take her to Audrey Hepburn and Grace Kelly movies to point out the outfits they wanted, just as their mothers had done with Joan Crawford and Katherine Hepburn movies. Judging from their expressions as they pirouetted before their image in their commissioned artwork, she never failed their expectations except perhaps for that occasional zipperless bride. She certainly never disappointed me as I sat in solemn and curious attention, peering into her face as I searched for some trace of how she had acquired her special powers.

There was another aspect to Amanda that only we seemed to whisper about, in very low tones, and that was that Amanda was dabbling in herbs. Although none of us considered her a real *hechicera* or enchantress, we always had reservations about drinking or eating anything she gave us, and although no one ever saw the proverbial little figurines, we fully suspected she had them hidden somewhere, undoubtedly decked out as exact replicas of those who had ever crossed her in any way.

Among her few real friends were two old women who came to visit her by night, much to everyone's consternation, for those two only needed one quick stolen look to convince you they were more than amateurs. Librada and Soledad were toothless old women swathed in black or brown from head-to-toe, and they carried their back sack filled with herbs and potions slung over their shoulder, just as *brujas* did in my books. They had a stare that seemed to go right through you, and you knew that no thought was secret from them if you let them look even once into your eyes.

One day, in the year when it rained without stopping for many days in a row and the puddles swelled up with more bubbles than usual, I found myself sitting alone in the screened-in porch admiring the sound of the fat raindrops on the roof; suddenly I looked up to find Librada standing there in her dark brown shawl, softly knocking on the door.

"The lady has sent a message to your mother," she said while my heart thumped so loudly its noise scared me even further. I managed to tell her to wait there, by the door, while I went to call my mother. By the time Mother came to check on the visitor, Librada was already inside, sitting on the couch, and since the message was that Amanda wanted Mother to call one of her customers to relay some information, I was left alone with the old woman. I sat on the floor pretending to work on a jigsaw puzzle while I really observed Librada's every move. Suddenly she broke the silence asking me how old I was and when my next birthday would be. Before I could phrase any words, Mother was back with a note for Amanda, and Librada was on her way. Sensing my tension, Mother suggested we go into the kitchen to make some good hot chocolate and to talk about what had just happened.

After I drank my cup, I came back to the porch, picked up one of my *Jack and Jill*'s, and lay on the couch. Then, as I rearranged a cushion, my left arm slid on a slimy greenish-gray substance and I let out such a screech that mother was at my side in two seconds. Angry at her for having taken so long to come to my aid, I kept wiping my arm on the dress and screaming, "Look at what that *bruja* has done." She very, very slowly took off my dress and told me to go into the shower and to soap myself well. In the meantime she cleaned up the mess with newspapers and burned them outside by the old brick pond. As soon as I came out of the shower, she puffed me up all over with her lavender-fragranced bath powder, and for the rest of the afternoon we tried to figure out what the strange episode had meant. Nothing much happened to anyone in the family during the following wet days, and mother insisted we forget the incident.

But I didn't forget it for a long time. On my next visit to Amanda's, I described in detail what had happened. She dismissed the entire episode as though it weren't important, shrugging, "Poor Librada. Why are you blaming her for what happened to you?"

With that, I went back to my silent observation, now suspecting she too was part of a complex plot I couldn't figure out. Yet, instead of making me run, incidents like these drew me more to her, for I distinctly sensed she was my only link to other exciting possibilities that were not part of the everyday world of the others. What they could be I wasn't sure of, but I was so convinced of the hidden powers in that house that I always wore my scapular and made the sign of the cross before I stepped inside.

After the rains stopped and the moon began to change colors, I began to imagine a dramatic and eerie outfit that I hoped Amanda would create for me. Without discussing it with my sisters, I made it more and more sinister, and finally, when the frogs stopped croaking, I built up enough nerve to ask her about it. "Listen, Amanda, could you make me the most beautiful outfit in the world? One that a witch would give her favorite daughter? So horrible that it would enchant everyone . . . maybe black with wings on it like a bat's."

She looked at me with surprise. "Why would you want such a thing?"

"Cross my heart and hope to die, I really won't try to scare anyone."

"*Pues, chulita,* I'm so busy right now, there's no way I can agree to make you anything. One of these days, when God decides to give me some time, I might consider it, but until then, I'm not promising anyone anything."

And then I waited. Dog days came and went, and finally, when the white owl flew elsewhere, I gave up on my request, brooding over my having asked for something I should have known would not be coming. Therefore, the afternoon that Veronica dropped off a note saying that *la señora* wanted to see me that night because she had a surprise for me, I coolly said I'd be there only if my mother said I could go.

II

All the time I waited to be let in, I was very aware that I had left my scapular at home. I knew this time that something very special was about to happen to me, since I could see even from out there that Amanda had finally made me my very special outfit. Mounted on a little-girl dress-dummy, a swaying black satin cape was awaiting my touch. It was ankle-length, with braided frogs cradling tiny buttons down to the knee. On the inside of the neckline was a black fur trim. "Cat fur," she confessed, and it tickled my neck as she buttoned the cape on me. The puffy sleeves fitted very tightly around the wrist, and on the upper side of each wristband was attached a cat's paw, which hung down to my knuckles. Below the collar, on the left side of the cape, was a small stuffed heart in burgundy-colored velveteen and, beneath the heart, she had sewn in red translucent beads.

As she pulled the rounded ballooning hood on me, rows of stitched-down pleats made it fit close to the head. Black chicken feathers framed my face, almost down to my eyes. Between the appliques of feathers, tiny bones were strung, which gently touched my cheeks. The bones came from the sparrows that the cats had killed out in the garden, she reassured me. She then suggested I walk around the room so she could take a good look at me.

As I moved, the cat's paws rubbed against my hands, and the bones of the sparrows bounced like what I imagined snowflakes would feel like on my face. Then she slipped a necklace over my head that was so long it reached down to my waist. It too was made of bones of sparrows strung on the finest glittering black thread, with little bells inserted here and there. I raised my arms and danced around the room, and the bells sounded sweet and clear in the silence. I glided about the room, then noticed in the mirror that Librada was sitting in the next room, and she was laughing under her breath. Without thinking, I walked up to her and asked what she thought of my cape.

"Nenita, you look like something out of this world. Did

you notice I just blessed myself? It scares me to think of the effect you are going to have on so many. *¡Que Dios nos libre!"*

I looked at Librada eye to eye for the first time, then felt that the room was not big enough to hold all the emotion inside of me. So I put my arms around Amanda and kissed her two, three, four times, then dramatically announced that I was going to show this most beautiful of all creations to my mother. I rushed outside, hoping not to see anyone on the street, and since luck was to be my companion for a brief while, I made it home without encountering a soul. Pausing outside the door of the kitchen where I could hear voices, I took a deep breath, knocked as loudly as I could, and in one simultaneous swoop, opened the door and stepped inside, arms outstretched as feathers, bones, and *cascabeles* fluttered in unison with my heart.

After the initial silence, my sisters started to cry almost hysterically, and while my father turned to comfort them, my mother came towards me with a face I had never seen on her before. She breathed deeply, then quietly said I must never wear that outfit again. Since her expression frightened me somewhat, I took off the cape, mumbling under my breath over and over how certain people couldn't see special powers no matter how much they might be staring them in the face.

I held the *bruja* cape in my hands, looking at the tiny holes pierced through the bones of sparrows, then felt the points of the nails on the cat's paws. As I fingered the beads under the heart, I knew that on that very special night when the green lights of the fireflies were flickering more brightly than usual, on that calm transparent night of nights I would soon be sleeping in my own witch's daughter's cape.

III

Sometime after the Judases were all aflame and spirals of light were flying everywhere, I slowly opened my eyes to a full moon shining on my face. Instinctively my hand reached to my neck, and I rubbed the back of my fingers gently against the cat's fur. I should go outside, I thought. Then I slipped off the bed and tiptoed to the back door in search of that which was not inside.

For a long time I sat on a lawn chair, rocking myself against its back, all the while gazing at the moon and the familiar surroundings, which glowed so luminously within the vast universe, while out there in the darkness, the constant chirping of the crickets and the cicadas reiterated the reassuring permanence of everything around me. None of us is allowed to relish in powers like that for long, though, and the vision of transcendence exploded in a scream as two hands grabbed me at the shoulders then shook me back and forth. "What are you doing out here? Didn't I tell you to take off that awful thing?"

Once again I looked at my mother in defiance but immediately sensed that she was apprehensive rather than angry and I knew it was hopeless to argue with her. Carefully I undid the tiny rounded black buttons from the soft, braided loops and took off the cape for what I felt would be the last time.

IV

Years passed, much faster than before, and I had little time left for dark brown-lavender puddles and fanciful white owls in the night. Nor did I see my cape after that lovely-but-so-sad, once-in-a-lifetime experience of perfection in the universe. In fact, I often wondered if I had not invented that episode as I invented many others in those endless days of exciting and unrestrained possibilities.

Actually, the memory of the cape was something I tried to flick away on those occasions when the past assumed the unpleasantness of an uninvited but persistent guest; yet, no matter how much I tried, the intrusions continued. They were especially bothersome one rainy Sunday afternoon when all the clocks had stopped working one after another as though they too had wanted to participate in the tedium of the moment. So as not to remain still, I mustered all the energy I could and decided to pass the hours by poking around in the boxes and old trunks in the storeroom.

Nothing of interest seemed to be the order of the afternoon when suddenly I came upon something wrapped in yellowed tissue paper. As I unwrapped the package, I uttered a sigh of surprise on discovering that inside was the source of the disturbances I had been trying to avoid. I cried as I fingered all the details on the little cape, for it was as precious as it had been on the one day I had worn it many years before. Only the fur had stiffened somewhat from the dryness in the trunk.

Once again I marvelled at Amanda's gifts. The little black cape was so obviously an expression of genuine love that it seemed a shame it had been hidden for all those years. As I carefully lifted the cape out of the trunk, I wondered why my mother had not burned it as she had threatened, yet knowing full well why she had not.

V

From then on, I placed the little cape among my collection of few but very special possessions that accompanied me everywhere I went. I even had a stuffed dummy made, upon which I would arrange the cape in a central spot in every home I made. Over the years, the still-crisp little cape ripened in meaning, for I could not imagine anyone ever again taking the time to create anything as personal for me as Amanda had done when our worlds had coincided for a brief and joyous period in those splendid days of luscious white gardenias.

When the end came, I could hardly bear it. It happened many years ago when the suitcase containing the little cape got lost en route on my first trip west. No one could understand why the loss of something as quaint as a black cape with chicken feathers, bones of sparrows, and cat's paws could cause anyone to carry on in such a manner. Their lack of sympathy only increased my own awareness of what was gone, and for months after I first came to these foggy coastal shores, I would wake up to *lentejuelas de concha nácar* whirling about in the darkness, just as they had done so long ago in that magical room in Amanda's house.

VI

Back home, Amanda is aging well, and although I haven't seen her in years, lately I have been dreaming once again about the enchantment that her hands gave to everything they touched, especially when I was very tiny and to celebrate our birthdays, my father, she, and I had a joint birthday party lasting three days. During this time, he would use bamboo sticks to make a skeletal frame for a kite, and then Amanda would take the frame and attach thin layers of marquisette to it with angel cords. In the late afternoon, my father would hold on to the cords, while I floated about on the kite above the shrubs and bushes; and it was all such fun. I cannot recall the exact year when those celebrations stopped, nor what we did with all those talismanic presents, but I must remember to sort through all the trunks and boxes in my mother's storeroom the next time that I am home.

Tomás Rivera

Tomás Rivera was born into a Chicano migrant family in 1935 in Crystal City, Texas. He grew up migrating back and forth from Texas to the Midwest until his first years in college. He earned bachelor's and master's degrees in Education, and later, a Ph.D. in Spanish literature. Since his childhood, Rivera was an avid reader, but he noticed that in mainstream literature, Hispanics had no representation. He incorporated his experiences as a migrant worker into his writing, portraying his struggles, and his socioeconomic and political hardships. In *...y no se lo tragó la tierra/...And the Earth Did Not Devour Him* (1971), Tomás Rivera depicted a search of identity of self and of people in the Mexican-American community. In 1970, *...y no se lo tragó la tierra* won the first national award for Chicano literature, the Quinto Sol Literary Prize, and was made into an award-winning motion picture, "And the Earth Did Not Swallow Him." While teaching English and Spanish in public high schools, and later also teaching at universities, Rivera always sought to voice the migrant workers' struggles and find justice for them through his writing. In 1976, Rivera became vice-president at the University of Texas in San Antonio; in 1978, at the University of Texas in El Paso, he became executive vice-president, and finally, in 1979, he became the first Mexican-American university chancellor in the United States at the University of California, Riverside. Rivera received international claim as one of the best Chicano writers, an educator and scholar who paved the way for other Mexican-American writers in their efforts to enrich Chicano literature.

from
...y no se lo tragó la tierra/
...And the Earth Did Not Devour Him

What his mother never knew was that every night he would drink the glass of water that she left under the bed for the spirits. She always believed that they drank the water and so she continued doing her duty. Once he was going to tell her, but then he thought that he'd wait and tell her when he was grown up.

∿∿
∿∿

The teacher was surprised when, hearing that they needed a button on the poster to represent the button industry, the child tore one off his shirt and offered it to her. She was surprised because she knew that this was probably the only shirt the child had. She didn't know whether he did this to be helpful, to feel like he belonged, or out of love for her. She did feel the intensity of the child's desire, and this was what surprised her most of all.

The Salamanders

What I remember most about that night is the darkness, the mud and the slime of the salamanders. But I should start from the beginning so you can understand all of this, and how, upon feeling this, I understood something that I still have with me. But I don't have this with me only as something I remember, but as something that I still feel.

It all began because it had been raining for three weeks and we had no work. We began to gather our things and made ready to leave. We had been with that farmer in Minnesota waiting for the rain to stop but it never did. Then he came and told us that the best thing for us to do was to leave his shacks because, after all, the beets had begun to rot away already. We understood, my father and I, that he was in fact afraid of us. He was afraid that we would begin to steal from him or perhaps that one of us would get sick, and then he would have to take the responsibility because we had no money. We told him we had no money, neither did we have anything to eat and no way of making it all the way back to Texas. We had enough money, perhaps, to buy gasoline to get as far south as Oklahoma. He just told us that he was very sorry, but he wanted us to leave. So we began to pick up our things. We were leaving when he softened up somewhat and gave us two tents, full of spider webs, that he had in the loft in one of his barns. He also gave us a lamp and some kerosene. He told my dad that if we went by way of Crystal Lake in northern Iowa, perhaps we would find work among the farmers and perhaps it had not been raining there so much and the beets had not rotted away. And we left.

In my father's eyes and in my mother's eyes, I saw something original and pure that I had never seen before. It was a sad type of love, it seemed. We barely talked as we went riding over the gravel roads. The rain seemed to talk for us. A few miles before reaching Crystal Lake, we began to get remorseful. The rain that continued to fall kept on telling us monotonously that we would surely not find work there. And so it was. At every farm that we came to, the farmers would only shake their heads from inside the house. They would not even open the door to tell us there was no work. It was when they shook their heads in this way that I began to feel that I was not part of my father and my mother. The only thing in my mind that existed was the following farm.

The first day we were in the little town of Crystal Lake everything went bad. Going through a puddle, the car's wiring got wet, and my father drained the battery, trying to get the car started. Finally, a garage did us the favor of recharging the battery. We asked for work in various parts of that little town, but then they got the police after us. My father explained that we were only looking for work, but the policeman told us that he did not want any gypsies in town and told us to leave. The money was almost gone, but we had to leave. We left at twilight, and we stopped the car some three miles from town, and there we saw the night fall.

The rain would come and go. Seated in the car near the ditch, we spoke little. We were tired. We were hungry. We were alone. We sensed that we were totally alone. In my father's eyes and in my mother's eyes, I saw something original. That day we had hardly eaten anything in order to have money left for the following day. My father looked sadder, weakened. He believed we would find no work, and we stayed seated in the car waiting for the following day. Almost no cars passed by on that gravel road during the night. At dawn I awoke and everybody was asleep, and I could see their bodies and their faces. I could see the bodies of my mother and my father and my brothers and sisters, and they were silent. They were faces and bodies made of wax. They reminded me of my grandfather's face the day we buried him. But I didn't get as afraid as that day when I found him inside the truck, dead. I guess it was because I knew they were not dead and that they were alive. Finally, the day came completely.

That day we looked for work all day, and we didn't find any. We slept at the edge of the ditch, and again I awoke in the early morning hours. Again I saw my people asleep. And that morning I felt somewhat afraid, not because they looked as if they were dead, but because I began to feel again that I no longer belonged to them.

The following day we looked for work all day again, and nothing. We slept at the edge of the ditch. Again I awoke in the morning, and again I saw my people asleep. But that morning, the third one, I felt like leaving them because I truly felt that I was no longer a part of them.

On that day, by noon, the rain stopped and the sun came out and we were filled with hope. Two hours later we found a farmer who had some beets that, according to him, probably had not been spoiled by the rain. But he had no houses or anything to live in. He showed us the acres of beets, which were still under water, and he told us that, if we cared to wait until the water went down to see if the beets had not rotted, and if they had not, he would pay us a large bonus per acre that we helped him cultivate. But he didn't have any houses, he told us. We told him we had some tents with us, and if he would let us, we would set them up in his yard. But he didn't want that. We noticed that he was afraid of us. The only thing that we wanted was to be near the drinking water, which was necessary, and also we were so tired of sleeping seated in the car, and, of course, we wanted to be under the light that he had in his yard. But he did not want us, and he told us, if we wanted to work there, we had to put our tents at the foot of the field and wait there for the water to go down. And so we placed our tents at the foot of the field, and we began to wait. At nightfall we lit up the lamp in one of the tents, and then we decided for all of us to sleep in one tent only. I remember that we all felt so comfortable being able to stretch our legs, our arms, and falling asleep was easy. The thing that I remember so clearly that night was what awakened me. I felt what I thought was the hand of one of my little brothers, and then I heard my own screaming. I pulled his hand away, and, when I awoke, I found myself holding a salamander. Then I screamed, and I saw that we were all covered with salamanders that had come out from the flooded fields. And all of us continued screaming and throwing salamanders off our bodies. With the light of the lamp, we began to kill them. At first we felt nauseated because, when we stepped on them, they would ooze milk. It seemed they were invading us, that they were invading the tent as if they wanted to reclaim the foot of the field. I don't know why we killed so many salamanders that night. The easiest thing to do would have been to climb quickly into our car. Now that I remember, I think that we also felt the desire to recover and to reclaim the foot of the field. I do remember that we began to look for more salamanders to kill. We wanted to find more to kill more. I remember that I liked to take the lamp, to seek them out, to kill them very slowly. It may be that I was angry at them for having frightened me. Then I began to feel that I was becoming part of my father and my mother and my brothers and sisters again.

What I remember most about that night was the darkness, the mud and the slime of the salamanders, and how hard they would get when I tried to squeeze the life out of them. What I have with me still is what I saw and felt when I killed the last one, and I guess that is why I remember the night of the salamanders. I caught one and examined it very carefully under the lamp. Then I looked at its eyes for a long time before I killed it. What I saw and what I felt is something I still have with me, something that is very pure—original death.

Jesús Salvador Treviño

Born in El Paso, Texas, in 1946, and later moving to Los Angeles when he was three years old, Jesús Salvador Treviño grew up among the Mexican-American community. He became greatly involved in the Mexican-American civil rights movement during the 1960s and 1970s, both participating in the movement as well as documenting the daily struggles faced by Hispanic students and workers alike. *Eyewitness: A Filmmaker's Memoir of the Chicano Movement* (2001) depicts a firsthand account of his experiences in the movement. In 1995, Treviño published his first collection of stories, *The Fabulous Sinkhole and Other Stories*, using his wit and humor to write about life in the Latino barrios. The collection was a finalist for the Publishers Marketing Association's 1996 Benjamin Franklin Award. Besides being a writer, Treviño is also a director and producer, who has received international recognition for his films. Among the television dramas he has directed and produced are: *NYPD Blue, Babylon 5, Star Trek: Voyager* and *Deep Space Nine, Chicago Hope,* and *Nash Bridges.* Through his pioneering filmmaking and writing, Treviño has helped Chicanos shape and define their Mexican-American identity.

The Fabulous Sinkhole

The hole in Mrs. Romero's front yard erupted with the thunderous whoosh of a pentup volcano, sending a jet of water dancing eight feet into the air. It stood there for a moment, shimmering in the sun like a crystal skyscraper, before it fell back on itself and settled into a steady trickle of water emanating from the earth.

The gurgling water made a soft, sonorous sound, not unlike music, as it quickly spread, inundating the low lawn surrounding the sculpted hole, painting a swirling mosaic of leaves, twigs, and dandelion puffs.

Pages of the weekly *Arroyo Bulletin News* were swept up by the fast-moving water, creating a film of literary discourse that floated on the surface of the water before becoming soaked and eventually sinking into the whirlpool created by the unusual hole.

Within moments of the unexpected appearance of the geyser, the serenity of Mrs. Romero's ordinary, predictable world was disrupted. On that Saturday morning Mrs. Romero's life, and that of the other residents of Arroyo Grande, a border town along the Rio Grande River, was forever transformed by an event as mysterious as the immaculate conception and as unexpected as summer snow.

The routine of Mrs. Romero's Saturday mornings—the leisurely watering of her philodendrons, Creeping Charlies, and spider plants, the radio recipe hour, and the morning *telenovelas*—evaporated the moment that she stepped out the back door to feed Junior, her three-year-old poodle/Afghan mix.

No sooner had she opened the door to the back yard, than the dog, whom she let sleep in the house with her, caught whiff of something and ran around to the front of the house. He bounded back in a moment and began to jump, yelp, whine, bark, and engage in other canine theatrics to draw Mrs. Romero's attention to something unusual that was happening in her front yard.

"*¿Qué trae ese perro?*" Mrs. Romero asked herself as she circled her house and walked out to the front of her modest stucco home. She then saw that Junior was barking at a hole in her front yard.

The hole was about three feet in diameter. It was located ten feet from the white picket fence that framed her front yard and a few yards from the cement walkway leading from her porch to the sidewalk.

As she walked down the porch steps, she noticed the most pleasant vanilla odor in the air. "*Qué bonito huele,*" she thought to herself.

She started to waddle across the lawn, but saw that it was flooded and opted to use the cement walkway instead. When she got to the point on the walkway that was closest to the hole, she stooped over to examine the depression and noticed that there was water bubbling up from the earth.

Mrs. Romero's first thought was that some of the neighborhood kids had dug the hole during the night. "*Chavalos traviesos,*" she surmised. But when she saw that there was water coming up from the ground, she had second thoughts about this being the mischievous work of local juveniles.

Where was the water coming from? Perhaps it was a broken water main. Just then, a clump of grass fell into the hole as it expanded further. The hole seemed to be growing.

"*Qué raro,*" she said as she stood up.

Mrs. Romero was not someone easily buffaloed by much of anything in her long and eventful life. She had weathered the deportations of the thirties (eventually returning to Arroyo Grande by foot, thank you), the Second World War, six children (all living), sixteen grandchildren, three husbands (deceased), four wisdom tooth extractions, an appendectomy, the blizzard of '52, an Internal Revenue audit, and weekly assaults on her privacy by Jehovah's Witnesses.

She was not about to be bamboozled by a mere hole in the ground.

She walked into her house and returned with a broom, which she proceeded to stick into the hole, handle first, to see if she could determine how far down the hole went.

When the broom handle had gone in to the point where she was holding the broom by the straw whiskers, she gave up and pulled the broom out. "What a big hole," she said out loud.

About this time, thirteen-year-old Reymundo Salazar, who lived in the adjacent block and was well known for the notorious spitball he pitched for the Arroyo Grande Sluggers, happened to be walking by Mrs. Romero's house on his way to Saturday-morning baseball practice. Seeing Mrs. Romero taking the stick out of the hole in the lawn, he stopped and asked what was up.

"*Mira, m'ijo,*" she said. "Come look at this hole that just now appeared *aquí en mi patio.*"

Reymundo opened the gate and entered the yard,

scratching Junior under his left ear. The dog by now had forgotten the mystery of the hole and was trying to get up a game of ball with the boy.

"Did you dig this hole, Señora?" Reymundo asked.

"*No, m'ijo,* that's the way I found it," Mrs. Romero said, somewhat defensively. She wiped her wet hands on the apron that circled her ample midriff and shook her head in wonder. "Look, it's getting bigger."

Sure enough, as Reymundo and Mrs. Romero watched, another large clump of earth fell into the hole as more and more water bubbled up from the earth below.

"You'd better get a plumber, Señora," advised Reymundo as he started back to the sidewalk, "It's probably a broken water pipe."

"*Ay Dios mío,*" said Mrs. Romero, shaking her head once again. "If it's not one thing, it's another."

As he walked away, Reymundo, who had been raised by his mother to be polite to older people, thought he'd compliment Mrs. Romero for the wonderful smell that permeated the air. He assumed it came from something she had doused herself with. "Nice perfume you're wearing, Mrs. Romero," he called out to her. "Smells real nice!"

♒

Within an hour, news of the hole in Mrs. Romero's front yard had spread throughout Arroyo Grande as neighbors from as far away as Mercado and Seventh Street came to see the sight. Mrs. Romero's next-door neighbors, Juan and Eugenia Alaniz, were the first over.

Mrs. Romero explained the appearance of the strange hole to the couple, and Juan said he'd see what he could find out. He went back to his garage and returned with a long metallic pole with which he began to plumb the depths of the sinkhole. Like young Reymundo, he was certain it was a broken water pipe and thought he might locate it with the metal pole.

But after much probing, and getting his worn Kinney casuals soaked, Juan reported back to Mrs. Romero that he could find no pipes under her yard. "Beats me," he said.

By now the hole had enlarged to about six feet across. More and more water kept bubbling up, undermining the earth around the edges of the hole until eventually another bit of the lawn went into the hole. It appeared to sink to a bottom. Juan Alaniz extended his twenty-foot measuring tape to its full length and stuck it into the hole, and still it did not hit bottom.

"It's deep," he said authoritatively to Mrs. Romero and his wife Eugenia, showing them the twenty-foot mark on the measuring tape. "Real deep."

"*Qué bonito huele,*" said Eugenia. "Smells like orange blossoms."

"No," said Juan, "smells like bread pudding. You know, *capirotada.*"

"Yes," said Mrs. Romero. "I noticed the smell, too. But it smells like vanilla to me. No?"

"Cherry-flavored tobacco," said grumpy Old Man Baldemar, who had crossed the street to see what the commotion was about. "It definitely smells of cherry-flavored tobacco."

Old Man Baldemar was known on the block for his foul mouth and his dislike of the neighborhood kids. He seldom spoke to anyone, kept to himself, and most people just stayed clear of him. That he would go out of his way to be social was just another indication of the deep feelings the hole stirred in those who saw it.

While Mrs. Romero and her neighbors discussed the powerful aroma that came from the hole, Reymundo Salazar returned from the baseball field along with the members of the Arroyo Grande Sluggers. They descended on Mrs. Romero's on their skateboards, looking like a swarm of fighter planes coming down *Calle Cuatro.* Reymundo had told his friends about the doings at Mrs. Romero's, and all were eager to see the mysterious water hole.

"Maybe it goes all the way to China!" Reymundo joked as he came to a stop in front of the white picket fence that surrounded Mrs. Romero's yard.

"Nah, a hole can't go all the way through the earth," said twelve-year-old Yoli Mendoza, taking it all very seriously as she finished off a perfect street-to-sidewalk ollie and came to a stop next to him. Yoli was advanced for her age, a real brain at school, and the tomboy of the group. She never missed a chance to show the boys in the neighborhood that she knew more about most things than they did, or that she could outskate them.

"In the center of the earth there's thick molten rock," she said professorially. "The *magma* and nothing can get through it—not even this hole."

At this point, chubby Bobby Hernández, also twelve years old but nowhere near Yoli's intellect, started arguing with Yoli, hoping to browbeat her into admitting that it *was* possible for a hole to extend from Mrs. Romero's yard all the way to China.

"Itcanitcanitcanitcanitcan," he said, as if repeating it

enough times would make it so.

"You are an ignoramus and a lout," Yoli said emphatically, adjusting the ribbon at the end of her ponytail, "and not worth the time it takes to argue with you."

"Maybe we'd better call the Department of Water and Power," said Juan Alaniz as he examined the hole. "I'll do that and see if they can't get somebody out here. After all, it's water—they should know what to do."

While Juan went off to his house to place the call, Eugenia and Old Man Baldemar stayed to talk to Mrs. Romero. Meanwhile, other neighbors on *Calle Cuatro* were beginning to gather to see what all the commotion was about.

Mrs. Domínguez, the neighborhood gossip, who had spied the crowd forming down the street and presumed there had been a car accident, immediately called Sally Méndez and Doña Cuca Tanguma and told them to meet her at Mrs. Romero's. When the three arrived and found there was no accident but only an ever-widening water hole, Mrs. González was only momentarily embarrassed.

"Why, this is much better than an accident," she said to her friends as she regained her composure, "because no one's been hurt."

Miguelito Pérez, driving to work at the Copa de Oro restaurant bar, pulled his '73 Chevy over when he saw the crowd on *Calle Cuatro,* and got out to investigate. Within moments he, too, was integrated into the crowd.

"Hey, Señora Romero," he said, pointing to the picket fence that separated the expanding hole from the cement sidewalk. "If this hole continues to grow, it's going to wreck your fence."

Don Sabastiano Diamante, an expatriate Spaniard who laced his conversation with Biblical quotations and aphorisms, heard the commotion as far away as *Calle Diez.* He found the long walk to Mrs. Romero's rewarded by an ideal opportunity to dazzle a few more souls with his knowledge of the Good Book. He was always quick to point out how the scriptures neatly underscored the socialist ideals that had led him in and out of the Spanish Civil War and eventually brought him to Arroyo Grande.

"And God said, Let the waters under the heaven be gathered together unto one place," Don Sabastiano quoted as he walked his dachshund Peanuts slowly around the body of water, *"and the gathering together of waters he called the Seas.* Genesis One, Ten."

Choo-Choo Torres, who would later give an account of the day's events to his sixth-grade class during the afternoon "Tell-a-Story" hour, arrived early on with the other Sluggers and made a list of the people who visited Mrs. Romero's front yard on that day.

Among the five pages of names that Choo-Choo Torres painstakingly compiled were: Old Man Baldemar, Don Carlos Valdez, Ed Carillo, Eddie Martínez, Cha Cha Mendiola, Juan and Eugenia Alaniz, Raúl and Simón Maldonado, Braulio Armendáriz, Pablo Figueroa, Raoul Cervantes, Sam Bedford (from the City Bureau of Public Works), the Méndez family (six in all), the Márquez Family (father and three kids), the Baca family (four in all), the Armenta family (eight in all), the Arroyo Grande Sluggers (eleven kids in all, including Reymundo Salazar, Bobby Hernández, Tudí Domínguez, Choo-Choo Torres, Beto Méndez, Robert and Johnnie Rodríguez, Junior Valdez, Smiley

Rojas, Jeannie De La Cruz, and, of course, Yoli Mendoza), Howard Meltzer (the milkman), Chato Pastoral, Kiki Sánchez, Richard and Diane Mumm (visiting from Iowa), Mrs. Ybarra, Mrs. Domínguez, Sally Méndez, Doña Cuca Tanguma, Dr. Claude S. Fischer (who was conducting a sociological survey of barrio residents), Rolando Hinojosa, Miguelito Pérez, Rosalinda Rodríguez, Mr. and Mrs. Alejandro Morales, Charles Allen (who connected Arroyo Grande homes with cable TV), Lefty Ramírez, the Cisneros family (nine in all), Don Sabastiano Diamante and his dog Peanuts, Julia Miranda, One-Eyed Juan Lara, Sylvia Morales, Rusty Gómez (from the Department of Water and Power), David Sandoval, Max Martínez, 'Lil Louie Ruiz, Rudy 'Bugs' Vargas, Pete Navarro, Bobby Lee and Yolanda Verdugo, the Torres family (four not counting Choo-Choo), Elvis Presley, Ritchie Valens, César Chávez, Frida Kahlo, John F. Kennedy, Che Guevara, Michael Jackson, and Pee Wee Herman.

The last several names, of course, were scoffed at by Choo-Choo's classmates. Yoli Mendoza, who sat two seats behind Choo-Choo, lost no time in openly accusing him of being a big fat liar, to which the other classmates joined in with a chorus of "yeahs" and "*órales.*"

Truth to tell, Choo-Choo *had* gotten a bit carried away with his list-making, but didn't see any need to admit his minor human idiosyncrasies to riffraff the likes of his classmates.

With brazen, deadpan bravado that—years later— would serve him in good stead at the poker table, Choo-Choo insisted that each and every one of the people on his list had been at Mrs. Romero's house that day, and that he had personally seen them with his own two eyes.

Had it been a weekday with everyone off to work, the crowd that gathered in front of Mrs. Romero's might not have been very big. But it was a Saturday morning, and quite a warm, sunny day at that. An ideal day for neighbors to come together and get caught up on each other's lives. And that they did.

By eleven o'clock that morning the crowd in front of Mrs. Romero's yard was easily more than fifty people and growing bigger and bigger by the hour.

For Mrs. Romero it was quite a delight. She had not had so many visitors in years, not since her husband, Maclovio, had passed away. Her husband's death had taken the spark out of Mrs. Romero's life—they had been married for thirty-six years—and no matter what her daughters, son, and grandchildren tried to do to cheer her up, her laughter always seemed forced and her smile polite. There were some who said she was merely biding time, waiting to join her husband. Her children, caught up in their own lives, came to visit less and less frequently. On the day of the sinkhole, it had been a long month since she had been visited by anyone.

But now, hearing the lively chatter from her neighbors, she wondered why she hadn't made more of an effort to get out and meet people *herself.*

She felt warmed by the company of her neighbors and the cheerful sound of their laughter. Then and there she resolved that from now on she'd make it a point to visit her neighbors on a regular basis and would demand that her children and grandchildren visit more often. "*¡Va!*" she thought to herself, "I'm not in the grave yet."

Tony Valdez, who ran the corner store, heard about the crowd gathering at Mrs. Romero's, and his money-making mind immediately sprang into action. He sent his son Junior, who made the mistake of returning from baseball practice to tell his dad about the doings at Mrs. Romero's, to the location with a grocery cart full of cold Cokes.

Before long, a *tamalero,* a *paletero,* and a fruit vendor had joined the boy, and all were doing brisk business in front of Mrs. Romero's house.

By noon there was quite a festive air to the day as neighbors sipped Cokes, munched tamales, chomped on popsicles, and carried on the kind of conversation they normally reserved for weddings and funerals. Old friendships were renewed, new friends made, and, in general, more gossip and telephone numbers exchanged that day than had been exchanged in months.

One-Eyed Juan Lara stopped to examine the crowd at the ever-widening hole and speculated that if the hole got any bigger, Mrs. Romero could charge admission for the neighborhood kids to swim in it.

"You'll have your own swimming pool, Señora," he said, "just like the *ricos.*"

Frank Del Roble, who had grown up on *Calle Cuatro* and now worked as a reporter for the real town newspaper, the *Arroyo Daily Times,* overheard Don Luis and countered that this probably wasn't such a good idea. "If this water is coming from a broken sewer line," he said, "the water might be contaminated, might get people sick."

"But look how clear it is," Juan Lara replied, pointing to the bubbling aperture.

Frank had to admit that the water flooding Mrs.

Romero's front lawn was quite clear and not at all looking like a sewage spill.

Frank had been driving to the office when he had seen the crowd gathered outside Mrs. Romero's and had gotten out to investigate. Now, he pulled out his trusty spiral notepad and began taking notes.

Bobby Hernández, meanwhile, was still contending that the hole went all the way to China, and Yoli was still arguing back that he was crazy, an ignoramus, and going against accepted scientific fact.

Bobby wasn't sure what an ignoramus was, but was damned if he was going to ask Yoli about it.

About this time a large "plop" sound announced the arrival of the first of many items that would bubble up in Mrs. Romero's front yard that day.

"Look!" Bobby said smugly, pointing to the hole. "I told you so!"

All heads turned to the hole, and a hush fell over the group of spectators as they stared in wonder at the item floating on top of the water.

To Yoli's astonishment and Bobby's delight, it was a large, straw hat, pointed in the center, not unlike those worn by millions of Chinese people halfway around the world.

〰〰
〰〰

"No, it's not a broken pipe," said Rusty Gómez, who worked for the Department of Water and Power and had been sent over to investigate the commotion on *Calle Cuatro*. He had measured and prodded the watery hole for half an hour before announcing his conclusion to the sizeable group gathered at Mrs. Romero's.

"What you have here," he said, "is a sinkhole!"

A murmur coursed through the crowd as they played the new word on their lips.

"What's a sinkhole?" Mrs. Romero asked. She was determined to know all about this thing that had disrupted her day and was creating such ever-widening chaos in her yard.

"It's a kind of depression in the ground; it caves in when undermined by water from an underground river or stream. You don't know it's there until the ground gives way and the water surfaces."

"Yeah?" said Juan Alaniz cautiously. "So where's the river?"

"Years ago," continued Rusty, "there used to be an arroyo going through this neighborhood, right along *Calle Cuatro*. When it rained, a good-sized stream used to run through here, right down to the Rio Grande. There's probably an underground stream some place, and that's where this water is coming from."

"That," Rusty mused, "or an underground cavern connecting to the Rio Grande itself. Hell, it's only a half mile away. Yeah, I'd say this water's coming from the Rio Grande."

"Well, what can I do about it?" Mrs. Romero asked.

"Don't know, Señora. If I were you, I'd call the City Bureau of Public Works. They've got an engineering department. This is more their field of work. Say, what is that, a bird cage?" Rusty Gómez pointed to the sinkhole where a shiny aluminum bird cage had suddenly popped up from the ground.

Old Man Baldemar, who lived alone in a single-room

converted garage, and whose only companions were two parakeets named *el gordo y el flaco,* fished the bird cage out of the water.

"Señora Romero," he said. "If you don't mind, I'd like to keep this here bird cage. The one I have for my *pajaritos* just this morning rusted through in the bottom. Those birds will get a real kick out of this."

"*Cómo no,* Señor Baldemar," Mrs. Romero replied. "If you can use it, *pos* take it!" And that is how the first of the articles that popped into Mrs. Romero's front yard was taken away by one of the residents of Arroyo Grande.

Within an hour, more and more items began to float to the surface of the sinkhole, now about fifteen feet across. Choo-Choo, Reymundo, Yoli, Bobby, and the rest of the neighborhood kids kept themselves busy by pulling objects out of the sinkhole and laying them on the sidewalk to dry.

Frank Del Roble, who had already gotten a couple of quotes from Mrs. Romero for the piece he was now sure he'd write on the event at *Calle Cuatro,* stooped over the sidewalk and started making a list of the artifacts.

Throughout the day, Frank kept a careful record of the items that came bubbling up through Mrs. Romero's sinkhole, and this is what the list looked like:

a brown fedora, size $7^1/2$,
fourteen football player cards, three of Joe Montana,
one baseball player card of Babe Ruth,
a Gideon bible,
a pair of plastic 3-D glasses,
a paperback edition of Webster's dictionary,
three paperback science-fiction novels,

four Teenage Mutant Turtle comic books,
a baseball bat,
three baseball gloves, one of them for a left-hander,
one basketball,
fourteen golf balls,
four unopened cans of semigloss paint primer,
an aluminum bird cage,
a 1975 world globe,
a tuba,
a yellow plastic flyswatter,
one yard of blue ribbon,
a toy magnifying glass,
a 1965 Smith Corona typewriter,
an April 1994 issue of *Art News* magazine,
a July 16, 1965, issue of *Life* magazine,
an August 1988 issue of *Life* magazine,
a July 4, 1969, issue of *Time* magazine,
the *Los Angeles Times* for October 9, 1932,
an issue of *TV Guide* magazine for the week of April 18–23, 1988
an unused package of condoms,
a blank certificate of merit,
fourteen Mexican coins of various denominations,
a three-peso Cuban note,
$3.17 in U.S. currency including a silver dollar,
a 500 yen note,
a size 14.5 steel-belted Goodyear radial tire,
the frame of a black, 1949 Chevy Fleetline,
a New York Mets baseball cap,
a deck of Hoyle playing cards with the ten of clubs and the three
    of diamonds missing,
a finely crafted silver pin,
a brochure for travel to Machu Picchu,
a claw-toothed hammer,

three screwdrivers,
a pair of compasses,
a ruler,
a leatherbound copy of *David Copperfield,*
three pairs of jeans,
sixteen shirts of different kinds, sizes, and colors,
a white terrycloth robe with the initials RR on it,
eight sets of men, and women's shoes,
a broken Mickey Mouse watch,
a 14K-gold wedding band,
a bronze belt buckle,
a fake pearl broach,
a tambourine,
three empty wine bottles made of green glass,
an orange pet food dish,
a wooden walking cane with a dragon carved on the handle,
two umbrellas, one bright red and one yellow with brown stripes,
a 20-foot extension cord,
32 empty soft drink bottles of assorted brands,
a pair of Zeitz binoculars,
a mint set of U.S. postage stamps commemorating rock and roll/
     rhythm and blues,
a Max Factor makeup kit,
five brand new #2 pencils,
a Parker fountain pen,
four ball-point pens,
a set of ceramic wind chimes,
six pairs of sunglasses, one with a lens missing,
the figures of Mary, the baby Jesus, Joseph, and a camel from a
     porcelain nativity scene,
a framed autographed photo of Carmen Miranda,
a bag of clothespins,
a three-speed Schwinn bicycle with one wheel missing,

six size C Duracell batteries,

six record albums: *La Jaula de Oro* by Los Tigres del Norte, a collection of "Top Hits from 1957," a Sesame Street Singalong
album, an album by The Jackson Five, "Learn to Mambo with
Pérez Prado," and The Beatles' White Album,

a black and red intergalactic laser gun with accompanying black
plastic communicator and extraterrestrial voice-decoder,

a sturdy, wooden push broom with a large bristle head,

an 8x10 wooden frame,

a red brick,

a map of Belkin County, Texas,

a book of Mexican proverbs,

a desk stapler,

two large black-and-white fuzzy dice,

a plastic swizzle stick with a conga dancer at one end, a rounded ball at the other end, and "Havana Club" printed along its
side,

a subway token,

a red-and-white packet of love potion labeled *"Medicina de Amor,"*

a 5x7 artist sketch pad,

five auto hubcaps, four of them matching,

a St. Christopher's medal,

a 4-inch metal replica of the Eiffel Tower,

a New York auto license,

a large ring of assorted keys,

a plastic hula-hoop, and lastly,

a Chinese sun hat.

As curious as Frank's exhaustive list was, the fact is that
by the end of the day every single article had found a home
in the hands of one or another of the people who stopped
by Mrs. Romero's.

In quite a number of cases, the article seemed ideally

suited for the person who picked it up, like Old Man Balde-mar walking away with a new bird cage for the one that had broken that morning, or Miguelito Pérez finding a hubcap to replace the one he had lost the week previous. Alejandro Morales found a red brick with the company name "Simons" embossed on it, and was inspired to use it as the centerpiece for the new brick front porch he was adding to his house.

In other cases, the link between what a person took away from the sinkhole and a particular need in his or her life was not apparent at all.

Tudí Domínguez, for example, walked away from Mrs. Romero's having collected all 32 soft drink bottles and intending to return them to a recycling center for the rebate.

But on the way home he ran into Marcy Stone, a blonde-haired, blue-eyed *gringuita* on whom he had a dev-astating crush, and, rather than be seen carrying the bag of empty bottles, dumped them in a nearby trash can. The bot-tles never surfaced again.

Marcy continued to ignore Tudí throughout sixth and seventh grade until her family moved out of town, and Tudí grew up to be a used-car salesman. Never once did he ever think of the Coke bottles he abandoned that day, nor was any of the four wives he married in the course of his other-wise uneventful life either blonde or blue-eyed.

For most people at Mrs. Romero's, it wouldn't be until weeks, months, or even years later that they would associ-ate an item they had carried off from the sinkhole on that peculiar Saturday with a specific influence in their lives.

By one o'clock, the sinkhole had undermined the earth on which Mrs. Romero's white picket fence was built and, just as Miguelito Pérez had predicted, the fence, pickets and all, plopped into the water.

Juan Alaniz helped Miguelito pull the picket fence out as a favor to *la señora,* and they neatly stacked the broken sections of the fence on her front porch.

Sam Bedford, from the City Bureau of Public Works, finally showed up at two o'clock that afternoon.

The balding city employee was grumpy because his afternoon game of golf had been disrupted by an emergency call to see about potholes on Fourth Street.

"Well, that's definitely more than a pothole," Sam said, whistling in astonishment at the sinkhole, which now measured twenty feet across.

By now the neighborhood kids had collected several dozen items and had them neatly drying on the sidewalk in front of Mrs. Romero's house.

The crowd had numbered about a hundred people as neighbors had continued to call friends and relatives to see the unusual event.

Sam strutted about the hole for about an hour, comparing the yard and the street with several city maps and sewage charts he carried under his arm. Now and then he'd say "uh-huh" or "yeah," as if carrying on a deep conversation with himself.

Finally he returned to Mrs. Romero's porch where the elderly woman sat sipping lemonade with Mrs. Domínguez, Sally Méndez, and Doña Cuca Tanguma.

"Don't know what to tell you, lady," Sam said, putting his maps away. "It sure looks like a sinkhole, though I've never seen one so large. We won't be able to do anything about it till Monday. I'll put in a request for a maintenance crew to come out here first thing."

"But what about in the meantime?" Mrs. Romero asked.

Sam just shook his head. "Sorry, I can't help you. Just keep people away so no one falls in." As he walked away, he noticed something amid the pile of junk that was accumulating on the sidewalk. "Oh, by the way," he continued, "do you mind if I take some of those golf balls laying over there?"

♒

If there were two incidents that would be remembered by everyone on the day of Mrs. Romero's sinkhole, it was the argument between Father Ronquillo and his parishioner Señora Florencia Ybarra, and the appearance of the largest item to pop out of the sinkhole, something that occupied the concentrated energy of five well-built young men and a tow truck for more than an hour.

The Father Ronquillo incident began innocently enough when Mrs. Ybarra, whose devotion to the Blessed Mother was renowned, saw a Gideon Bible pop out of the sinkhole. She fished it out of the water and found, to her amazement, that although the leatherette cover of the book was wet, when she opened it up, the inside pages were on the whole pretty dry.

She examined the Bible carefully and came to a conclusion she immediately shared with her assembled neighbors.

"It's a miracle!" she said, waving the Bible in the air. "Look, *la Santa Biblia* is dry! This water hole is a sign from the Lord and this Bible proves it!"

Mrs. Domínguez and several other women gathered about Mrs. Ybarra to examine the Bible. They all agreed that the Bible, though damp, should have been soaked, and that some divine intervention was not out of the question.

What capped the argument was the sudden appearance of a porcelain figure of Mary from a nativity scene, followed in swift succession by a porcelain baby Jesus and a porcelain Joseph.

"*¡Milagro!*" The mummur spread through the crowd.

Father Ronquillo, dressed in his workout sweats and out on his morning jog, happened by Mrs. Romero's at precisely this moment. The crowd spent little time ushering him to the sinkhole to witness for himself the Holy Bible and figurines of the Blessed Mother, Joseph, and the baby Jesus that had miraculously appeared in the water.

"Oh, thank God you are here, Father," Mrs. Ybarra said. "Look, it's a miracle!"

The parish priest was silent for a moment as he examined the figures and the still-widening sinkhole. He listened to Rusty Gómez's explanation of the sinkhole, then talked with Sam Bedford, then listened once again to Mrs. Ybarra, and then examined the figurines.

He hadn't counted on facing a theological debate on his morning jog, but was only too eager to shoulder his life work responsibly when the challenge presented itself.

"Well, there's certainly nothing miraculous about this," he said, pointing to the undersides of the figures. "Look, it says J.C. Penney." He passed the figurines around for everyone to examine, and, sure enough, the store name was printed on price labels stuck to the underside of each figurine.

"Of course it's no miracle," Frank Del Roble said emphatically as he compiled his list of the objects assembled on the sidewalk. Frank's university education had trained him to loathe superstitious people. "It's what keeps the barrio down," he was often heard to say. "Superstition and religion and no respect for science."

He surveyed the sizeable collection laid out on the sidewalk. "I think Rusty's right. This stuff's probably been dragged here by some underground current of the Rio Grande. There's a scientific explanation for everything."

"It's from South America, that's what!" said Bobby Hernández. "The Rio Grande is connected to the Amazon. I betcha all these things come from down south!"

"The Rio Grande definitely does *not* connect to the Amazon," Yoli countered, only too eager to show off her knowledge of geography. "The Rio Grande starts in Colorado and empties into the Atlantic Ocean in the Gulf of Mexico."

"It *is* connected to the Amazon," Bobby replied, secretly convinced that Yoli made up the facts that she announced with such authority. "Itisitisitisitisitis!"

"*Es un cuerno de abundancia,*" said Don Sabastiano. "It's a cornucopia bringing something for everyone here."

"Definitely the Rio Grande," Juan Alaniz said, ignoring Don Sabastiano and nodding to Father Ronquillo. "That would explain where all this stuff is coming from." He picked up a silver dollar from the collection of artifacts laid out on the sidewalk and flipped it in the air. "All this stuff is probably from some junk yard up river."

Father Ronquillo, however, was not eager to allow the faith of his parishioners to be dispelled so easily. After all, if their faith was allowed to be undermined on these little matters, where would it end?

"There is a scientific explanation for everything," he agreed, examining a 20-foot extension cord that had been drying on the sidewalk. He remembered that the parish needed one.

"But remember that our Lord invented science." He turned to the crowd around him and assumed his best clerical demeanor, at least the best he could dressed in jogging sweats.

"All of this may come from some junk yard," he said, putting the extension cord under the elastic of his jogging pants, "but that doesn't mean that some higher power did not arrange for all of this to happen."

"Then it *is* a miracle," said Mrs. Ybarra, feeling vindicated.

"For those who believe, there will always be miracles," he said with reassuring eloquence. "And those unfortunate souls so tainted by the cynicism of the world that they cannot believe," he eyed Frank Del Roble pointedly, "are only the lesser for it."

"I still think that all this stuff is coming from South America," said Bobby, not giving up.

"I must prepare for the afternoon Mass," Father Ronquillo said, moving through the crowd and back on his running route. "Mrs. Romero," he said as he passed her, "you should call the city to see about filling in this hole before it does much more damage."

Indeed by now the hole had expanded to the edge of the walkway and sidewalk. There, the cement had put a halt to its growth. But on the far side of the yard, where there was no cement, the hole had gone on a gluttonous rampage, devouring so much of Mrs. Romero's front yard that when Don Sabastiano paced off the hole, it measured fully forty feet across. It was enormous by any standard. It now appeared it might endanger Mrs. Romero's house.

Father Ronquillo's none-too-subtle barb at Frank Del Roble had left the reporter muttering under his breath. "Superstitious fools, that's what," he reiterated to himself.

Frank's dream was to work someday for the *Los Angeles Times,* a newspaper of record with an enormous readership that Frank considered worthier of his considerable journalistic talents than the few thousand readers of the *Arroyo Daily News.* Frank believed that his strict adherence to scientific truth was his ticket to the big time.

As if to prove to himself and those around him that he was not in the least bit superstitious, he challenged in a voice loud enough for everyone in the crowd around him to hear, "If this is a miracle, may the earth open up and swallow me!"

No sooner had the words left his mouth, then a deep reverberation began in the ground immediately underneath Frank. The journalist's face blanched white as the whole area around Mrs. Romero's front yard began to tremble and rock, knocking several people off their feet and forcing everyone to struggle for balance.

Don Sabastiano, who in his many travels had experienced more than his share of life's wonders, immediately called out a warning to his neighbors. "Hold on to something, it's an earthquake!"

But an earthquake it was not. For just as quickly as it had started, the shaking subsided and was replaced by a loud rumbling sound rolling from under the sinkhole. While Frank caught his breath, reassured that the ground on which he stood was firm, the attention of the crowd was focused on the sinkhole as water began spouting up into the air.

The rolling rumble grew to a crescendo. When the noise had risen to a level that caused people to hold their hands over their ears, the sinkhole emitted a deafening whoosh.

With a power that sent water spraying a hundred yards in all directions, the sinkhole suddenly belched up the full frame of a 1949 black Chevy Fleetline.

♒

"Get the hook around the front bumper," seventeen-year-old Pete Navarro called out as he stuck his head out of the cab of his Uncle Mickey's tow truck. It was four o'clock in the afternoon, an hour after the appearance of the 1949 Chevy Fleetline.

Rudy Vargas, Pete Navarro, David Sandoval, 'Lil Louie Ruiz, and Arroyo Grande teenagers whose reputations were murky but who never actually been caught doing anything illegal, had agreed to haul the car out of Mrs. Romero's yard as a favor to *la señora* and for whatever parts they might strip from the vehicle.

As they prepared to haul the car, which looked like a giant bloated cockroach, out of the sinkhole, they discovered to their surprise that it was in remarkably good shape for having been completely submerged in water for who knows how long.

"Look," said Rudy, sitting atop the roof of the car still floating in the middle of the sinkhole, "it's a little rusty, but this chrome can be polished up." The steady bubbling of water from under the sinkhole seemed to keep the car afloat.

"We give it a new paint job," he continued, "replace the engine, some new upholstery, and this could be quite a nice ride."

"Doesn't look like it was in the water very long at all," 'Lil Louie agreed, sipping a Coke as he sat on Mrs. Romero's porch. Somehow, when Rudy, Pete, David, and Louie undertook enterprises, it was always Rudy, Pete, and David who wound up doing the work, and 'Lil Louie who managed to oversee the operation. "My managerial talents at work," he would explain.

The neighbors of Arroyo Grande gawked in wonder at the durable automobile defying the laws of nature by floating on the surface of the sinkhole. The water line went up to the car wheels.

"All set?" Pete cried out.

"*¡Dale!*" Rudy replied.

With a lurch, Pete began to edge the tow truck away from the sinkhole, slowly turning the car on its axis in the water and bringing it up to the shore of what could now be properly called the pond in Mrs. Romero's front yard.

The crowd watched with anticipation as the cable on the tow truck lifted the front end of the Fleetline out of the water. "Let me get off," yelled Rudy as he jumped off the hood of the car.

Pete waited until Rudy was clear and then continued to lift the car out of the water and over the sidewalk. But then the lifting stopped.

The tow truck alone could not get the Chevy's back wheels onto the sidewalk where Mrs. Romero's white picket fence had been. The car's upper end was in the air and its bottom end in the sinkhole.

"Come on guys," said Rudy to the men in the crowd, "*pasen mano.*"

Miguelito Pérez, Rudy Vargas, David Sandoval, Frank

Del Roble, and 'Lil Louie gathered themselves under the car and began to push extra hard from below as Pete tried the lift again. Slowly the Chevy's rear end rose out of the water. The men shoved some more, each one straining to the limit of his strength.

Finally, the car's rear wheels touched the sidewalk.

It was a dramatic moment, and the crowd could not help but give out a collective "Ah" as the back wheels of the vehicle caught hold of the ground. Within seconds Pete was driving the tow truck down the street, dragging the dripping Chevy behind it.

"*¡Gracias a Dios!*" Mrs. Romero said. "I don't know how I would have gotten that thing out of there. You boys, *son tan buenos muchachos.*"

As the commotion of the Chevy Fleetline's departure quieted down, Choo-Choo Torres noticed something along the edge of the sinkhole's water line.

He called Frank Del Roble over, and the two conferred in whispers for a moment. Frank took a stick and held it against the side of the hole for a moment and then nodded to Choo-Choo that he was right. Choo-Choo turned to the crowd and announced loudly, "Mrs. Romero. Look! The water's going away!"

Mrs. Romero and her neighbors gathered at the edge of the pond and saw that, sure enough, like the water in a sink when the plug is pulled, the water in her sinkhole seemed to be receding slowly into the depths of the earth.

The Chevy Fleetline had been the last item to come out of the sinkhole, and now it seemed as if some master magician had decided that the show was over and it was time to go home.

Indeed, with the sun now low in the sky, people began to remember those things they had set out to do on that Saturday before the commotion at Mrs. Romero's had distracted them—the shopping, the wash, the mowing of the lawn, the repairs around the house. One by one, Mrs. Romero's neighbors began to drift away.

"*Adiós,* Señora Romero," said Mrs. Domínguez as she and her friends Sally and Doña Cuca left the sinkhole. They each carried something from the sinkhole: Mrs. Domínguez, a fake pearl broach and a bright red umbrella; Sally, a yellow-and-brown umbrella and a pair of harlequin-style sunglasses; and Doña Cuca, a set of ceramic wind chimes and a book of *adivinanzas.* They were joined by Bobby Lee Verdugo, who had picked up a shiny brass tuba, and his wife Yolanda, who had picked up an old issue of *Life* magazine and a tambourine. A noisy and colorful spectacle they all made walking up *Calle Cuatro* together, Bobby blowing notes on the tuba, Doña Cuca tapping the wind chimes, and Yolanda banging the tambourine in time to the music.

"*Sí, hasta luego,*" said Juan Alaniz, flipping the silver dollar he had picked up earlier. Eugenia, his wife, carried off a pile of shirts and a bag of shoes. "For the homeless," she had explained earlier. "I'll drop them by the Goodwill on Monday."

Fearful that she would have to call a trash man to haul away what remained of the collection of artifacts, Mrs. Romero urged her neighbors to take what they wanted home. "*¡Llévenselo todo!*" she said, "take anything you want!"

Don Sabastiano complied by carting off a sturdy wooden push broom with a wide bristle head.

Ed Carillo took a couple of old magazines that caught his eye. Thirty-five-year-old spinster Rosalinda Rodríguez took a white terrycloth robe with her initials on it. The robe fit her perfectly, which was surprising since the poor woman was constantly ridiculed for being the most over-weight person in Arroyo Grande.

Don Carlos Vásquez, who owned the Copa de Oro bar as well as several empty lots in Arroyo Grande, took a deck of Hoyle playing cards and a ring of assorted keys.

Twenty-two-year-old Julia Miranda, a dark-haired beauty who had been voted Most Likely to Succeed by her high-school graduating class, and whose ambition was to someday star in a Hollywood movie, took an autographed photo of Carmen Miranda, a pair of sunglasses, and a New York subway token.

No one really took note of who took what from the sinkhole—except perhaps when seven-year-old Moises Armenta walked up to his mother with an unopened package of condoms.

With the adults in the crowd chuckling, Mrs. Armenta quickly took the condoms from the child and put them in her purse, where they remained for several weeks until discovered by her husband Arnulfo when he was rifling through her purse looking for cigarette money.

By six that evening, when the street lamps began to go on up and down *Calle Cuatro,* all the items except for an orange dog food dish, a yellow flyswatter, and the Pérez Prado album had been taken away.

It was then that Mrs. Romero remembered that the whole day had started with her going into the back yard to feed Junior, and that in the course of the day's confusion she had forgotten to do that.

She looked out at her watery front yard, lit up by the street lights, and considered herself lucky.

The accidental appearance of the sinkhole had disrupted the mundane pattern of her daily activities and had given her a new appreciation for life. She wasn't sure what, if anything, it had done for her neighbors—but what a nice day it had turned out to be for her! Mrs. Romero was not an overly philosophical person, but as she stood on her porch watching the evening wrap itself around the modest houses of *Calle Cuatro,* she did have to wonder about the day's events.

Perhaps it was the mysterious workings of God, as Father Ronquillo had suggested. Or perhaps it was some other playful, magical force that had nudged her life and that of her neighbors. Or perhaps it was simply the overflow of the Rio Grande through a junk yard, all of it quite explainable by science.

Whatever the case, she was tired of thinking about it and eager to get on with the Pedro Infante movie, *Nosotros los pobres,* scheduled for TV that night. "Come on, Junior," she said, picking up the food dish, the flyswatter, and the album. "*Pobrecito,* it's time we got you some breakfast."

Pat Mora

Poet, writer, educator, and literary activist, Pat Mora was born in El Paso, Texas, in 1942. She studied and graduated from Texas Western College and the University of Texas at El Paso. After receiving her B.A. and M.A. degrees, Mora began teaching secondary and college level courses. Later she started writing and has since become an advocate for the conservation, not only of ecology, but also of culture, language, and traditions across the southwestern United States, bringing families and communities together through literature and learning. Mora's numerous children's books and collections of poetry cater to young readers and adults. Some of her works include the poetry collections *Chants* (1984), *Communion* (1991), the anthology, *My Own True Name: New and Selected Poems for Young Adults, 1984–1999* (2000), the children's books *The Bakery Lady / La señora de la panadería* (2001) and *Maria Paints the Hills* (2002), and her memoir, *House of Houses* (2002). Mora's diverse writing has made her a renowned author, receiving numerous awards and recognitions. Mora regularly gives poetry readings, lectures and workshops at schools, conferences and universities.

Fences

Mouths full of laughter,
the *turistas* come to the tall hotel
with suitcases full of dollars.

Every morning my brother makes
the cool beach sand new for them.
With a wooden board, he smooths
away all footprints.

I peek through the cactus fence
and watch the women rub oil
sweeter than honey into their arms and legs
while their children jump waves
or sip drinks from long straws,
coconut white, mango yellow.

Once my little sister
ran barefoot across the hot sand
for a taste.

My mother roared like the ocean,
"No. No. It's their beach.
It's their beach."

Line 2: Tourists.

Same Song

While my sixteen-year-old son sleeps,
my twelve-year-old daughter
stumbles into the bathroom at six a.m.
plugs in the curling iron
squeezes into faded jeans
curls her hair carefully
strokes Aztec blue shadow on her eyelids
smooths Frosted Mauve blusher on her cheeks
outlines her mouth in Neon Pink
peers into the mirror, mirror on the wall
frowns at her face, her eyes, her skin,
not fair.

At night this daughter
stumbles off to bed at nine
eyes half-shut while my son
jogs a mile in the cold dark
then lifts weights in the garage
curls and bench presses
expanding biceps, triceps, pectorals,
one-handed push-ups, one hundred sit-ups
peers into the mirror, mirror and frowns too.

for Libby

Tomás Rivera

They knew so much, his hands
spoke of the journey from Crystal City
to Iowa, Michigan, Minnesota, year after year
dirt-dusted in fields and orchards,
his hands a pillow at night,
in bare, cold buildings,
family laughter his favorite blanket.

On slow days his hands
gathered books at city dumps,
saved like the memories of smiling
hard at that first grade teacher
and her noises in the other language
that didn't laugh like Spanish.

Those hands clenched in the dark
at *víboras, víboras* hissing
  we don't want you, you people have lice
as the school door slammed
but Tomás learned,
and his hands began to hold books
gently, with affection. He searched
for stories about his people and finally
gave their words sound, wrote the books
he didn't have, we didn't have.

And he graduated over and over
until one day he was Chancellor Rivera,
famous Chicano, too needed,
his hands too full of us
to sit alone and write green stories
alive with voices, "fiesta of the living,"
pressing, the present pressing
like the hands reaching out to him,
and he'd hug the small, brown hands,
his hands whispering his secret
            learn, learn
his face a wink, teasing out their smiles,
a face all could rest in,
like the cherries he picked, dark,
sweet, round a pit, tooth-breaker
for the unwary, the lazy, the cruel.

His hands knew about the harvest,
tasted the laborer's sweat in the sweet
cantaloupes he sliced, knew how to use
laughter to remove stubborn roots
of bitter weeds: prejudice, indifference,
the boy from Crystal City, Texas,
not a legend to be shelved,
but a man whose *abrazos* still warm
us yet say, "Now you."

Title: Texas-born educator and author (1935–1984) of the novel *...y no
    se lo tragó la tierra.* (...And the Earth Did Not Devour Him) and
    other works.
Line 15: Snakes.
Line 47: Hugs, embraces.

Helena María Viramontes

Helena María Viramontes was born on February 26, 1954, in East Los Angeles to Chicano parents. She grew up among family members, friends, and even some strangers who would take refuge in her home, coming across the border from Mexico. From these adventurers Viramontes heard stories that would later inspire her writing. While studying at Immaculate Heart College, she started writing poetry and fiction, and graduated with a B.A. in English. She went to the University of California at Irvine and received an M.F.A. degree in creative writing and fiction. Viramontes, passionately proud of her Mexican-American heritage, depicts in her writing the social and cultural value of Chicanos, the struggles they face, and the failures and triumphs in their life experiences. Viramontes has published several novels and short stories, including the novels *Their Dogs Came with Them* (1996), *Under the Feet of Jesus* (1995), and the collection of short stories *The Moths and Other Stories* (1985). *The Moths and Other Stories* explores Latino women's struggles to survive and overcome the patriarchal Hispanic culture in which they live. She has also written a screenplay, "The Rats in East L.A.," which was produced by the American Film Institute in 1991. She is currently an assistant professor of English at Cornell University, Ithaca, New York.

Growing

The two walked down First Street hand in reluctant hand. The smaller one wore a thick, red sweater, which had a desperately loose button that swung like a pendulum. She carried her crayons, humming "Jesus loves little boys and girls" to the speeding echo of the Saturday-morning traffic, and was totally oblivious to her older sister's wrath.

"My eye!" Naomi ground out the words from between her teeth. She turned to her youngest sister who seemed unconcerned and quite delighted at the prospect of another adventure. "Chaperone," she said with great disdain. "My EYE!" Lucía was chosen by Apá to be Naomi's chaperone. Infuriated, Naomi dragged her along impatiently, pulling and jerking at almost every step. She was fourteen, almost fifteen, the idea of having to be watched by a young snot like Lucía was insulting to her maturity. She flicked her hair over her shoulder. "Goddammit," she murmured, making sure that the words were soft enough so that both God and Lucía could not hear them.

There seemed to be no way out of the custom. Her arguments were always the same and always turned into pleas. This morning was no different. "Amá," Naomi said, exasperated but determined not to cower out of this one, "Amá, the United States is different. Here girls don't need chaperones. Parents trust their daughters." As usual Amá turned to the kitchen sink or the icebox, shrugged her shoulders, and said: "You have to ask your father." Naomi's nostrils flexed in fury as she pleaded. "But, Amá, it's embarrassing. I'm too old for that. I am an adult." And as usual, Apá felt different, and in his house she had absolutely no other choice but to drag Lucía to a sock hop or church carnival or anywhere Apá was sure a social interaction was inevitable. And Lucía came along as a spy, a gnat, a pain in the neck.

Well, Naomi debated with herself, it wasn't Lucía's fault, really. She suddenly felt sympathy for the humming little girl who scrambled to keep up with her as they crossed the freeway overpass. She stopped and tugged Lucía's shorts up, and although her shoelaces were tied, Naomi retied them. No, it wasn't her fault after all, Naomi thought, and she patted her sister's soft light brown almost blondish hair; it was Apá's. She slowed her pace as they continued their journey to Jorge's house. It was Apá who refused to trust her, and she could not understand what she had done to make him so distrustful. *TÚ ERES MUJER,* he thundered like a great voice above the heavens, and that was the end of any argument, any question, because he said those words not as a truth, but as a verdict, and she could almost see the clouds parting, the thunderbolts breaking the tranquility of her sex. Naomi tightened her grasp with the thought, shaking her head in disbelief.

"So what's wrong with being a mujer," she asked herself out loud.

"Wait up. Wait," Lucía said, rushing behind her.

"Well, would you hurry? Would you?" Naomi reconsidered: Lucía did have some fault in the matter after all, and she became irritated at once at Lucía's smile and the way her chaperone had of taking and holding her hand. As they passed El Gallo, Lucía began fussing, hanging on to her older sister's waist for reassurance.

"Stop it. Would you stop it?" She unglued her sister's grasp and continued pulling her along. "What's wrong with you?" she asked Lucía. I'll tell you what's wrong with you, she thought, as they waited at the corner of an intersection for the light to change: You have a big mouth. That's it. If it wasn't for Lucía's willingness to tattle, she would not have been grounded for three months. Three months, twelve Saturday nights, and two church bazaars later, Naomi still hadn't forgiven her youngest sister. When they crossed the street, a homely young man with a face full of acne honked at her tight purple pedal pushers. The two were startled by the honk.

"Go to hell," she yelled at the man in the blue-and-white Chevy. She indignantly continued her walk.

"Don't be mad, my little baby," he said, his car crawling across the street, then speeding off, leaving tracks on the pavement. "You make me ache," he yelled, and he was gone.

"GO TO HELL, goddamn you!" she screamed at the top of her lungs, forgetting for a moment that Lucía told everything to Apá. What a big mouth her youngest sister had, for chrissakes. Three months.

Naomi stewed in anger when she thought of the Salesian Carnival and how she first met a Letterman senior, whose eyes, she remembered with a soft smile, sparkled like crystals of brown sugar. She sighed deeply as she recalled the excitement she experienced when she first became aware that he was following them from booth to booth. Joe's hair was greased back and his dimples were deep. When he finally handed her a stuffed rabbit he had won pitching dimes, she knew she wanted him.

As they continued walking, Lucía waved to the Fruit Man. He slipped off his teeth, and, again, she was bewildered.

"Would you hurry up!" Naomi told Lucía as she had told her that same night at the carnival. Joe walked beside them and took out a whole roll of tickets, trying to convince her to leave her youngest sister on the ferris wheel. "You could watch her from behind the gym," he had told her, and his eyes smiled pleasure. "Come on," he said, "have a little fun." They waited in the ferris wheel line of people.

"Stay on the ride," she finally instructed Lucía, making sure her sweater was buttoned. "And when it stops again, just give the man another ticket, okay?" Lucía said okay, excited at the prospect of heights and dips and her stomach wheezing in between. After Naomi saw her go up for the first time, she waved to her, then slipped away into the darkness and joined the other hungry couples behind the gym. Occasionally, she would open her eyes to see the lights of the ferris wheel spinning in the air with dizzy speed.

When Naomi returned to the ferris wheel, her hair undone, her lips still tingling from his newly stubbled cheeks, Lucía walked off and vomited. She vomited the popcorn, a hot dog, some chocolate raisins, and a candied apple. And all Naomi knew was that she was definitely in trouble.

"It was the ferris wheel," Lucía said to Apá. "The wheel going like this over and over again." She circled her arms in the air and vomited again at the thought of it.

"Where was your sister?" Apá had asked, his voice raising.

"I don't know," Lucía replied, and Naomi knew she had

just committed a major offense, and Joe would never wait until her prison sentence was completed.

"Owwww," Lucía said. "You're pulling too hard."

"You're a slowpoke, that's why," Naomi snarled back. They crossed the street and passed the rows of junk yards and the shells of cars, which looked like abandoned skull heads. They passed Señora Núñez's neat, wooden house, and Naomi saw her peeking through the curtains of her window. They passed the Tú y Yo, the one-room dirt pit of a liquor store where the men bought their beers and sat outside on the curb drinking quietly. When they reached Fourth Street, Naomi spotted the neighborhood kids playing stickball with a broomstick and a ball. Naomi recognized them right away, and Tina waved to her from the pitcher's mound.

"Wanna play?" Lourdes yelled from center field. "Come on, have some fun."

"Can't," Naomi replied. "I can't." Kids, kids, she thought. My, my. It wasn't more than a few years ago that she played baseball with Eloy and the rest of them. But she was in high school now, too old now, and it was unbecoming of her. She was an adult.

"I'm tired," Lucía said. "I wanna ice cream."

"You got money?"

"No."

"Then shut up." Lucía sat on the curb, hot and tired, and began removing her sweater. Naomi decided to sit down next to her for a few minutes and watch the game. Anyway, she wasn't really that much in a hurry to get to Jorge's. A few minutes wouldn't make much difference to someone who spent most of his time listening to the radio.

She counted them by names. They were all there. Fifteen of them, and their ages varied just as much as their clothes. They dressed in an assortment of colors, and looked like confetti thrown out in the street. Pants, skirts, shorts were always too big and had to be tugged up constantly, and shirt sleeves rolled and unrolled, and socks colorfully mismatched with shoes that did not fit. But the way they dressed presented no obstacle for scoring or yelling foul, and she enjoyed the abandonment with which they played. She knew that the only decision these kids made was what to play next, and for a moment she wished to return to those days.

Chano's team was up. The teams were oddly numbered. Chano had nine on his team because everybody wanted to be on a winning team. It was an unwritten law of stickball that anyone who wanted to play joined in on whatever team they preferred. Tina's team had the family faithful six. Of course, numbers determined nothing. Naomi remembered once playing with Eloy and three of her cousins against ten players, and still winning by three points.

Chano was at bat, and everybody fanned out far and wide. He was a power hitter, and Tina's team prepared for him. They could not afford a home run now because Piri was on second, legs apart, waiting to rush home and score. And Piri wanted to score at all costs. It was important for him because his father sat watching the game outside the liquor store with a couple of his uncles and a couple of malt liquors.

"Steal the base," his father yelled. "Run, *menso*." But Piri hesitated. He was too afraid to take the risk. Tina pitched, and Chano swung, missed, strike one.

"Batter, batter, swing," Naomi yelled from the curb. She stood to watch the action better.

"I wanna ice cream," Lucía said.

"Come on, Chano," Piri yelled, bending his knees and resting his hands on them like a true baseball player. He spat, clapped his hands. "Come on."

"Ah, shut up, sissy." This came from Lourdes, Tina's younger sister. Naomi smiled at the rivals. "Can't you see you're making the pitcher nervous?" She pushed him hard between the shoulder blades, then returned to her position in the outfield, holding her hand over her eyes to shield them from the sun. "Strike the batter out," she screamed at the top of her lungs. "Come on, strike the *menso* out!" Tina delivered another pitch, but not before going through the motions of a professional preparing for the perfect pitch. Naomi knew she was a much better pitcher than Tina. Strike two. Maybe not. Lourdes let out such a cry of joy that Piri's father called her a dog.

Chano was angry now, nervous and upset. He put his bat down, spat in his hands and rubbed them together, wiped the sides of his jeans, kicked the dirt for perfect footing.

"Get on with the game," Naomi shouted impatiently. Chano tested his swing. He swung so hard that he caused Juan, Tina's brother and devoted catcher, to jump back.

"Hey, *baboso,* watch out," Juan said. "You almost hit my *coco*." And he pointed to his forehead.

"Well, don't be so stupid," Chano replied, positioning himself once again. "Next time, back off when I come to bat."

"*Baboso,*" Juan repeated.

"Say it to my face," Chano said, breaking his stance and turning to Juan. "Say it again so I can break this bat over your head."

"Ah, come on," Kiki, the shortstop, yelled. "I gotta go home pretty soon."

"Let up," Tina demanded.

"Shut up, *marrana,*" Piri said, turning to his father to make sure he heard. "Tinasana, *cola de marrana.* Tinasana, *cola de marrana.*" Tina became so infuriated that she threw the ball directly at his stomach. Piri folded over in pain.

"No! No!" Sylvia yelled. "Don't get off the base or she'll tag you out."

"It's a trick," Miguel yelled from behind home plate.

"That's what you get!" This came from Lourdes. Piri did not move, and although Naomi felt sorry for him, she giggled at the scene just the same.

"I heard the ice-cream man," Lucía said.

"You're all right, Tina," Naomi yelled, laughing. "You're A-O-K." And with that compliment, Tina took a bow for her performance until everyone began shouting and booing. Tina was prepared. She pitched, and Chano made the connection quick, hard, the ball rising high and flying over Piri's, Lourdes's, Naomi's and Lucía's heads and landing inside the Chinese cemetery.

"DON'T JUST STAND THERE!!" Tina screamed to Lourdes. "Go get it, stupid." After Lourdes broke out of her trance, she ran to the tall chain-link fence that surrounded the cemetery, jumped on it with great urgency, and crawled up like a scrambling spider. When she jumped over the top of the fence, her dress tore with a rip-roar.

"We saw your *calzones,* we saw your *calzones,*" Lucía sang.

"Go! Lourdes, go!" Naomi jumped up and down in

excitement, feeling like a player who so much wanted to help her team win, but was benched on the sidelines for good. The kids blended into one huge noise, like an untuned orchestra, screaming and shouting, Get the ball, Run in, Piri, Go Lourdes, go, Throw the ball, Chano pick up your feetthrowtheballrunrunrunthrow the ball. *"THROW* the ball to me!!" Naomi waved and waved her arms. She was no longer concerned with her age, her menstruations, her breasts that bounced with every jump. All she wanted was an out at home plate. To hell with being benched. "Throw it to me," she yelled.

In the meantime, Lourdes searched frantically for the ball, tiptoeing across the graves saying, excuse me, please excuse me, excuse me, until she found the ball peacefully buried behind a huge gray marble stone, and she yelled to no one in particular, CATCH IT, SOMEONE CATCH IT. She threw the ball up and over the fence, and it landed near Lucía. Lucía was about to reach for it when Naomi picked it off the ground and threw it straight to Tina. Tina caught the ball, dropped it, picked it up, and was about to throw it to Juan at home plate when she realized that Juan had picked up home plate and run, zigzagging across the street while Piri and Chano ran after him. Chano was a much faster runner, but Piri insisted that he be the first to touch the base.

"I gotta touch it first," he kept repeating between pants. "I gotta." The kids on both teams grew wild with anger and encouragement. Seeing an opportunity, Tina ran as fast as her stocky legs could take her. Because Chano slowed down to let Piri touch the base first, Tina was able to reach him, and with one quick blow, she thundered OUT! She made one last desperate throw to Juan so that he could tag

Piri out, but she threw it so hard that it struck Piri right in the back of his head, and the blow forced him to stumble just within reach of Juan and home plate.

"You're out!!" Tina said, out of breath. "O-U-T, out."

"No fair!" Piri immediately screamed. "NO FAIR!!" He stomped his feet in rage. "You *marrana,* you *marrana.*"

"Don't be such a baby. Take it like a man," Piri's father said as he opened another malt liquor with a can opener. But Piri continued stomping and screaming until his shouts were buried by the honk of an oncoming car and the kids obediently opened up like a zipper to let the car pass.

Naomi felt like a victor. She had helped once again. Delighted, she giggled, laughed, laughed harder, suppressed her laughter into chuckles, then laughed again. Lucía sat quietly, to Naomi's surprise, and her eyes were heavy with sleep. Lucía wiped her eyes, looked at Naomi. "*Vamos,*" Naomi said, offering her hand. By the end of the block, she lifted Lucía and laid her head on her shoulder. As Lucía fell asleep, Naomi wondered why things were always so complicated once you became older. Funny how the old want to be young and the young want to be old. She was guilty of that. Now that she was older, her obligations became heavier both at home and at school. There were too many expectations, and no one instructed her on how to fulfill them, and wasn't it crazy? She cradled Lucía gently, kissed her cheek. They were almost at Jorge's now, and reading to him was just one more thing she dreaded, and one more thing she had no control over: it was another one of Apá's thunderous commands.

When she was Lucía's age, she hunted for lizards and played stickball with her cousins. When her body began to bleed at twelve, Eloy saw her in a different light. Under the house, he sucked her swelling nipples and became jealous when she spoke to other boys. He no longer wanted to throw rocks at the cars on the freeway with her, and she began to act differently because everyone began treating her differently, and wasn't it crazy? She could no longer be herself, and her father could no longer trust her because she was a woman. Jorge's gate hung on a hinge, and she was almost afraid it would fall off when she opened it. She felt Lucía's warm, deep breath on her neck, and it tickled her.

"Tomorrow," she whispered lovingly to her sister as she entered the yard. "Tomorrow I'll buy you all the ice creams you want."

Sarah Cortez

A proud native Houstonian, Sarah Cortez has loved writing since she was five years old. Cortez remembers cherishing the exchange of letters with an aunt and her delight in realizing that her writing was important enough for someone to treasure. Through several careers, Cortez never lost interest in writing, and in the 1980s took several creative writing courses, but it was in 1992 that she became a serious poet. As a police officer, fear, sensuality, denial, and the sense of a rush from a fast-paced job inspired Cortez's writing. A graduate from Rice University, the University of Texas, and the University of Houston, she has had work widely published in several literary journals and policing magazines. *How to Undress a Cop* is her first published collection of poetry. In 1999, she was the winner of the PEN Texas Literary Award for Poetry, and in 2000 she was named semifinalist in the Fourteenth Annual Louisiana Literature Prize for Poetry. Cortez taught as Visiting Scholar at the University of Houston's Center for Mexican American Studies (CMAS), and also served on the Latino Faculty Council. She currently juggles her career as a police officer, a writer, and an educator, teaching as an adjunct professor at CMAS, University of Houston.

Haunt

We girls sang Mass;
boys were altar boys.
Every morning before school
single file, silent,
hands folded in prayer
we marched into the Church.

Once during Mass
a flying shape—quick and small—
darted in a window. It was dark.
I think, scared. It circled
the glittering altar with its candles
then flew up into our choir loft.

We were in the middle
of a song. Sister pumping the organ
with tiny feet in laced black leather
against wood. It landed
on one girl's beanie. Too disciplined
to react, I chanted memorized Latin staring

only at the hummingbird. Then
Roseanne, the tall girl with glasses, reached,
placed her hand over the emerald bird's flutter,
caught it. Trapped, it squealed
once. She took it outside, down
the stairs, let it go. I still hear it.

Muffled in her hand. Hurt.
Surprised, and struggling.

Walking Home

I know who and what
will be there
when I arrive.

Mom chopping for dinner.
Attic fan cooling. Small
white dog, tail furled, barking.

Daddy will come home.
At dinner I'll drink two glasses
of ice-cold milk. We'll talk.

I'll fall asleep beneath saints'
smiles after homework,
dishwashing, praying on knees.

I cannot go back. Can you?
Can you walk home? Everyone
dead or simply grown up.

Remember each detail, its beauty.
Survive the memory, its nearness.

Walk yourself home, then back here again.

Mike Padilla

A second-generation Mexican American, Mike Padilla was born in Oakland in 1964. From an early age he began to develop a knack for telling stories, and lies, so he says, that developed into a great talent as he grew up. He studied Creative Writing at Stanford and Syracuse Universities. *Hard Language* (2000) is Padilla's first book of short stories, stories inspired by the diverse Hispanic population of California, stories that tell of the search for a better life. Padilla's writing deals with the compelling issues of cultural assimilation, as well as the non-assimilation of Mexican Americans to the North American culture on either side of the U.S.-Mexico border. *Hard Language* is the recipient of the 1997 San Francisco Foundation Joseph Henry Jackson Literary Award and winner of the University of California at Irvine's 1996–1997 Chicano/Latino Literary Prize. He has most recently received a California Arts Council Artists Fellowship in Literature. Padilla lives and writes in Los Angeles, California.

Carrying Sergei

When I was fourteen, my parents made their living selling six varieties of tamales, the best ones in town, at the edge of the tourist district on the Avenida Revolución. My job before every sunrise was to spread the dough and tie the corn husks while my mother cleaned the leaves. I gave my work my full attention, measuring out equal portions of dough and shaping the tamales into neat, plump oblongs. I always worked in a room by myself. My family and I got along better that way.

On the morning I was to meet Sergei Mikhailovich before school, I only wanted to finish as quickly as I could. Sergei had bet me 2,000 pesos that he could beat me in a race up Obregón Hill, and I was eager to collect my winnings. Sergei was new to Tijuana and could not have known that I was the only girl in the sixth grade who could scale all 364 steps by twos without stopping.

On the other side of the curtain that separated us, my mother's voice rose to a screech. "Get in there and help your sister. You're a big girl now. You're old enough to be of some use."

"Keep her out of my way," I yelled. "I'm in a hurry. I'll make her cry. I mean it."

"Everyone in this family can be of use," Mamá said.

"She's barely seven," I said.

"When you were seven, you did everything."

"I was exceptional."

"Exceptional girls don't talk back to their mothers. They don't start arguments with all the neighborhood."

"Señora Pacheco called me a thief. I had to defend myself."

"You didn't have to kick over her *tomatillos.* You didn't have to call her a *bruja vieja.*"

I was on the verge of shouting, but I caught myself. My parents had allowed me to take a year off from school to help with the family business, but now that I was back in school, I seemed to be getting into arguments daily. Benita Rubio had told me how humiliating it was for her to be seen with someone who was always shouting, even in ordinary conversation. For a week I had been trying to break myself of the habit.

A few minutes later, Mamá tried to drag Alicia through the doorway, but Alicia grabbed the doorframe with both hands. "I'm giving you one last chance," Mamá said.

"Or else what?" I said, thumping out a mound of dough. "I've told you before, if you want her to obey, you have to threaten her."

Alicia lost her grip. She grabbed the curtain instead, pulling down the curtain and rod with a crash. I stood up, and she squealed as I lifted her with one hand onto the stool next to mine.

"Put the tamales in boxes. Don't play with them. Be quiet."

When I had finished the last dozen tamales, I took off my apron and wiped my hands. I quietly plucked the daily sales ledger from the shelf above the stove and thumbed through the month's figures. I wasn't allowed to touch it, but Mamá often miscalculated, and I liked to check the totals for accuracy. Sure enough, I caught a mistake on the first glance. It was a wonder my father agreed to let her run the business while he was out of town. Her voice was too puny to attract customers above the horn-blaring downtown clamor, she often counted out change wrong, and she made the tamales twice as big as they had to be to appeal to the tourists. For a year I had been suggesting that we make them in two sizes, one for regular customers, and a smaller size for the Americans, who were always grinning as if there were nothing but bargains to be found in Tijuana.

I fixed the mistake, then leaned the ledger against the coupon jar at the same tilt I had found it.

"Did you finish your letter to Papá?" she said from the other room.

"I have to go," I said, reaching for my books on the stove burner. She came in, arms heaped to her chin with husks. She had gotten some of the silky yellow fibers in her hair. I went over and started to pick them out for her. She never looked in a mirror, and often went out into public with a dab of dough on her cheek or an earring missing from one ear. I got all the fibers out, but there was nothing I could do about her wispy drifts of hair.

On the way out I said, "Did you know you look very pretty?"

From the sink she looked over her shoulder at me as if a stranger had wandered into her kitchen.

"Benita thinks so, too," I said.

"Thank you, Margarita. That's a fine compliment."

I back-stepped, one foot out the door.

"I'll bet if you pulled your hair out of your face, and

tied it back . . ."

"Margarita! Did you finish your letter to Papá or not?"

"If you just bought some ribbon . . ."

"Do you want me to read it for you?"

"I already mailed it."

"I didn't give you a stamp."

"I got one from Benita."

"I thought you hated Benita."

"What?" I said, but I was already halfway out the yard.

"You hate Benita Rubio!"

I bounded over the slumped diamond-link fence, scaring up the chickens in the neighbor's back yard. I didn't think I was asking much of my mother, only that she not be the untidiest woman in our district. Any day now my father was going to write for us to join him in Sacramento, California, where he was setting up a food-distributing business with Tío Ramón, who was already a U.S. citizen. As much as my insides tightened at the thought of moving to a place with such a harsh-sounding name, I hoped we could at least do it without drawing attention to ourselves.

Not drawing attention to myself was something I was becoming an expert at. Over the last year I had burst out of my girlish proportions, gaining inches over my classmates in height and in the breadth of my shoulders. I had packed onto my frame a new density of flesh that left speechless the relatives who hadn't seen me recently. Girls like me, my teacher told me over and over, were prone to attract attention, which explained why I was always getting into fights. I needed to take extra care to speak softly, move cautiously, and use my smile to distract upward. As I made my way through neighbors' back yards, I was careful not to raise too much dust. I took figs only from the trees of houses where I knew no one was home.

At Benita's house I went around to the front and tapped at the screen.

Her mother appeared, strangling a broom handle with both hands. "Benita doesn't want anything to do with you," she said.

"Good morning, Señora Rubio," I said, giving the slightest curtsey. Though Benita and I spent more time being enemies than friends, I had always liked her mother's enchanting eyes.

She turned sharply and I went in. I looked around the room at her mother's paintings of French landscapes and hand-embroidered sofa covers. I wished that some day we would have such nice things, but Papá said the next few years were going to be full of sacrifices. I had only the bleakest picture of life in Sacramento. Benita told horrible stories about her second cousin Luz, who had been cheated out of her savings by an American who had promised to marry her. She had become a maid in Anaheim and had had to travel by bus two hours each morning to clean a ten-room house where only one person lived. She had finally killed herself, Benita said, by locking herself in one of four bathrooms and mixing together in a sink all the most toxic cleaning chemicals she could find.

Benita bulleted out of her own room on a direct course for the door. "You can walk with me if you want, but don't expect me to be pleasant." The screen slammed behind her.

I caught up with her down the block. "I need you to time the race for me today. I think I can beat my old record."

Benita swung her books close to her side in swift, angry jerks, eyes straight ahead. Her polished black shoes flashed sharply in the sun with each step.

"Can I carry your books for you?" I reached for them, but she pinched them more tightly under her arm.

A few moments passed. Then she blurted out, "I never thought I would be caught cheating."

"You were supposed to miss two or three problems on purpose," I said. "Everyone knows you're not smart enough to get the same score as me in science."

"I'm not stupid," Benita said.

"In some things, you are very stupid."

"You're going to kill yourself on those steps."

"I have excellent balance."

"Look at what happened to Rico Candelario."

"He was blind in one eye."

"My mother says to have nothing to do with you."

"A lot of mothers say that."

After a few minutes, I added, "I'll give you a quarter of the money I win. Five hundred pesos."

"We'll see," she said. "It depends."

"Seven-fifty," I pressed.

"I said it depends."

What it depended on, I knew, was whether Marisol Cruz and Gloria Rivera were already at school or not. These were the girls that had recently made room for Benita in their privileged and dangerous circle, taking her with them to their meeting place along the ocean and giving her cigarettes to smoke. With their rich, tempestuous hair and eyes that looked on everything with smoldering disdain, they were beyond popularity, as if that were a childish stage they had abandoned long before they had ever cracked their first pack of cigarettes. Benita was careful not to spend too much time with me when they had her in sight.

After a few minutes, she slowed her pace and sighed. "I suppose I should be tolerant of you. After all, when you leave, life for you isn't going to be easy."

"You don't know how it is," I said, faking enthusiasm. "Life in Sacramento is going to be fantastic. I'm going to have whatever I want."

For the rest of the way, I tried to copy her dainty, turned-in steps, the way she smiled at people she didn't know. When we passed Alfredo Zúñiga's house, she smiled and giggled to him on the porch. I did the same after her. I angled my books against my side the way she did. I swung my hips in the same rhythm.

I felt ridiculous. I sprinted out in front of her through the Colonia General Estrada. I took a leap at a limb of the peach tree, threaded my legs up through my arms like a gymnast, and swung upside-down until she caught up with me.

The Obregón School came into view on the distant hill that shot up at the downtown's western edge. It was a grim, looming, two-story building that looked more like a penitentiary than a public school. I was back for my final year, older than my classmates and a half foot taller than any teacher. Rules and restrictions and teachers' threats no longer intimidated me. As long as I kept to myself, both students and teachers left me alone.

But the most important thing I had conquered didn't lie inside its walls and corridors. It was the steep concrete steps that rose hazardously an eighth of a mile up the hill. Fifty-two broad steps led to the first plateau, then another fifty-two to the next, and so on all the way to the smog-hazy summit. I had raced these steps hundreds of times, and my growth spurt of the last year had pushed me to the top rank of racers. But because of my new effort to stand out less, I only raced if money was involved.

Benita stopped, scanned the top of the hill before we moved forward.

I nearly split open with laughter when I saw my opponent squatting on the bottom step. Sergei's thumbs were hooked into the enormous side pockets of adult-sized work pants that were bunched and cinched at his waist with rope. They were held together with so many different-colored patches that you couldn't tell where the pants began and the patches ended. He wore shoes with no socks, and his arms, skinny as curtain rails, jutted out of a shirt that was secured with every variety of button and even a safety pin where the collar button should have been. I was raised better than to laugh at the poor, but I wasn't laughing at him because he was poor. I was laughing because there was no way this humped, scrubby boy in clumsy clown clothes and hard-soled shoes had a chance to win against me.

"Did you bring the money?" I said. He smiled up at me and nodded. The few times I had heard him speak, it was with an accent, the words gurgling in his throat like gravel swirling in a sink drain. His family had moved here from Russia under circumstances Profesora Ruiz had never been able to get him to talk about. She had tried to get us to draw him out with questions about Russia, but people had just stared at him. General interest in him had lasted about three minutes.

I started doing body-twists to get limber.

"You'd better warm up," I said. "You don't want to tear a ligament."

He jumped up awkwardly like a broken stick puppet, started doing side-twists as well. I started doing deep knee bends. He did deep knee bends. I started running in place. So did he.

"Stop it," I said. "You can't do everything I do."

He stuck his hands back in his pockets, grinned at me stupidly. I sighed, shook my head. He had no idea how I was about to humiliate him.

"All right," I said. "Let's get started."

Benita took out her expensive watch with the built-in stopwatch that she was always showing off and started zigzagging up the hill. She was hardly recognizable when she got to the top. Marisol and Gloria must have been nowhere in sight, because she started yelling through cupped hands: "Attention, attention! Gather around, students of the Obregón School for the race of the century. Margarita Navarrete will race the insidious communist in a contest for world supremacy. It's the event you don't want to miss!"

I didn't know what a communist was or what insidious meant, but I appreciated her ability to stir up a crowd. If you were going to humiliate someone, the humiliation might as well be public and therefore complete.

I put my right foot on the bottom step. Sergei did the same.

Benita raised her hand. "Four. Three. Two. One . . ."

We launched up the steps before she said "go." I took the first set of them at an easy pace, letting the blood fill my legs. I let Sergei stay a few steps ahead of me. I let my mind unravel, threads of thought reaching out and touching whatever they wanted to. Then, slowly, I started to pull them in.

I started taking the steps by twos. I brought my breathing into rhythm with my legs, two strides for every breath in, two for every breath out. The cold air was like a knife stabbing into my lungs, but I didn't fight it. When I saw Sergei's footing start to get sloppy, I pulled my mind down into myself. At the third tier I shot up from behind and passed him.

By the fourth tier, the throbbing in my heart was like a fist punching the inside of my chest. The ache in my legs was fire burning up the wicks of my muscle fibers. The pain, I remembered, was not my opponent. I got down into the empty center that the pain seemed to come from. In a final white burst that had nothing to do with physiology, I exploded up the last steps to the top.

The group at the top of the hill was bigger than I had guessed.

"You did it," Benita said. "You beat your own time by four seconds."

I threw my arms overhead like a prizefighter. I kicked dirt up from the pavement. I whooped and hollered and jumped from foot to foot.

Sergei straggled up the steps a half-minute later, a gasping, perspiring, heaving jumble of bones and rags and patches. He had given up somewhere on the fourth incline, and was still pumping air too hard to speak. He didn't seem to notice kids laughing at him. He just stood there, puffing and sweating and smiling.

Smiling. I couldn't believe it. I had won by the biggest

margin ever, and he didn't seem to realize it. I repeated my victory dance. I whooped even louder. "You lost!" I said.

He kept smiling at me stupidly.

"I said, you lost! You're the loser. Are you stupid? Don't you understand?"

That smile was the most maddening thing I had ever seen. Crooked, translucent teeth, like pieces of broken eggshell, fought each other for space in the mosaic of his grin. He didn't try to insult my size or accuse me of cheating like boys usually did when they lost. He was being what no other boy I had raced had ever been. A good sport. And it was making me furious.

"Say something," I said. "Don't just stand there."

The school bell rang out furiously. Kids began ambling off, but I didn't move. I gazed hard at Sergei's dusty walnut hair, at the rings of pasty dirt around his neck. I didn't care if I got yelled at for being late. I was going to wring some satisfaction out of my victory. I was going to make him act like the loser he was.

I held his eye until I finally saw his smile quake. How stupid he was, I thought, to stand there with his back to the steps. If I were to shove him, he would have nothing to hold onto. I wouldn't even have to shove that hard, just give a slight push, a tap on the shoulder . . .

I don't know why I did it. It was hardly a push at all, just the merest brushing of my palm against his protruding collarbone, as if I were brushing away a piece of lint. But it was enough to tip him backwards, skinny arms helplessly rotating out at his sides, eyes peeling as he slowly but completely lost balance and fell, like a leaf from a tree arching backwards over itself in slow, continuous motion, until he lay in silence near the bottom of the top tier.

I ran to the front of the school and grabbed Profesora Ruiz. She must have seen in my face that something was wrong, for she immediately began to run in the direction I had come from. She plunged down the steps towards Sergei, hips bouncing, heavy wool dress swirling about her legs.

Sergei lay thirty steps down, like a pile of colorful laundry. I couldn't see his face. I couldn't tell his arms from his legs. I started to say something, but the whiteness of Profesora Ruiz's face when she looked up struck the words out of me. A light drizzle started. She threw her keys up to me and told me to unlock the classroom and tell the other students to wait for her there.

In the classroom the chatter of students filled the air, but from my seat in the back right corner, everything sounded muffled as if through glass. Benita and Marisol and Gloria had pushed their desks together and were huddled close in gossip. No one seemed to notice that anything was wrong, although Sergei's empty seat in the center of the room was to me like the gaping eye of a whirlpool that I was fighting not be sucked down into for the thing I had done.

Lies started to fill my head. I hadn't pushed him. He had slipped. We had been wrestling. He had been showing off. I hadn't seen anything. It was his word against mine.

I knew I would never be able to repeat one convincingly, but they kept filling my head like water rushing into a sinking boat. I was going down in a whirl of wretchedness and guilt and fear, the whole room spinning around me with not so much as a fiber of hope to grasp.

It seemed like an hour before the teacher came back, pale and spent, wringing a handkerchief on which I was sure I saw blood. She said that an ambulance had taken Sergei to the Catholic hospital, but that he would be fine. When no one pressed her for more, she opened a notebook to read from, but her voice choked. She dismissed us, pulling the door open as she stepped out into the hall.

There was a rush for the door, but I didn't move. I gripped the sides of my desk. I waited for her interrogation.

Several minutes passed, and she still hadn't come back into the room. I went to the door and looked out. There was no sign of her. There was no sign of anyone up or down the hall.

I stepped out quietly. I made my way slowly to the exit, my criminal's heart pounding. I stepped out into the light rain.

I ran. I ran down the steps, taking a dangerous six-step leap past the place where Sergei had fallen, down La Segunda to the bottom of the hill and past the banks and stores of the tourist district, then out into the wide, blank Bulevar Agua Caliente. I ran with a force I had never run with before, perilously fast across the slick pavement, the rain stinging my face, out to where the boulevard funneled into a dusty road beading with rain but not yet muddy. I ran with a speed that had nothing to do with trying to get somewhere and had everything to do with escaping my guilt, as if the earth were spinning nightmarishly fast beneath me.

The house was empty when I got home. It was still morning, but the clouds gave the room the weary feeling of late afternoon. I paced, rain and sweat sizzling down my face and arms, my skirt sticking to my legs. Consequences began to bear down on me. Benita's mother would forbid her from seeing me. She would tell the other mothers in the neighborhood, and everyone would be talking. I would be kicked out of my school and sent to some other, terrible school in Tijuana where they still practiced corporal punishment. And that was if the police didn't get involved. The tragic lives of Benita's cousins would be nothing compared to what was going to happen to me.

I stopped pacing and tried to catch my breath. There was still the possibility that Sergei would say nothing. But the only way that seemed likely was if he were dead. And if I were to wish for such a thing, how could I ever live with myself?

The rain thudded louder and louder on the windows as the afternoon stretched on. I looked for chores to do to make the time go faster, but the dishes were washed, and the floor had been swept. When my mother came home, I could not bear to be in the same room with her. I skipped dinner and went to bed early.

I waited for sleep to take me away, but sleep would not come. Each time I was about to drift off, I would think I heard someone at the door talking to my mother and I would jolt awake.

Late into the night my sister stirred next to me as I got out of bed. In the kitchen I dug out a sheet of paper from one of the cabinets. Quickly, but firmly, I wrote,

Dear Papá,

I am writing to say that I am very excited about moving to the United States. I know I have complained in the past about not wanting to go, but I have changed a lot since you last saw me and I realize that moving is the best thing for us. I beg for you to send for us as soon as possible.

I would be more than happy to come ahead of Mamá and Alicia if you think I can be of use.

Love, your adoring daughter,
Margarita

The next morning Mamá said she was feeling ill and wanted me to take over for her downtown after I had finished in the kitchen. Getting out of school that day was like a small, brilliant miracle. I got a stamp from her, left the house early, and mailed my letter at the first mailbox I saw.

Downtown was especially crowded, with tourists thronging the sidewalks and cars blaring horns futilely in clogged traffic. At first I was glad for the distraction, but soon I thought I saw people looking at me everywhere. I found myself giving out incorrect change and getting yelled at by locals who thought I was trying to cheat them. Just after three o'clock a police car came screaming up the street. I held my breath and crouched behind the register until it passed. Another hour must have gone by before I noticed that someone had stolen over ten thousand pesos from the till. I closed the stand up early and made my way home, exhausted and on the verge of tears.

Mamá wasn't feeling any better the next day, and I was able to put off returning to school through the weekend. But by Sunday, my misery was unbearable. Benita, whom I might at least have confided in, had not come by once. My crime was now common knowledge.

The day I was to go back to school, I got my chores over with early. I thought about skipping school for a few more days, hoping that miraculously my father would write for me to join him before I got caught. But the thought of another day alone was worse than the thought of facing what was coming.

Leaving the house, I cleared my thoughts the way I did before a race. I went the long way around the neighborhood to avoid running into anyone I knew.

I was the first one to arrive on the school grounds. I locked myself in a stall in the girls' room on the north side of the building, listening to the chatter beginning to grow outside. A half-hour later the bell screamed out. I waited until I didn't hear a voice. When I was sure all of the students were in their seats, I unlocked the stall. I made my entrance.

I went to my seat at the back of the class without looking at anyone. I could tell everyone was looking at me. Profesora Ruiz wasn't there yet.

Profesora Ruiz swept into the room. The door banged shut behind her, as if on my future. I put my head on my desk. I waited for her to address me.

"Let's begin today's class with a short science lesson," she began.

I peered over my forearms.

"Over the weekend did anyone hear about the satellite the Russians put into orbit around the earth?"

I lifted my head. I looked around. "What happened to Sergei?" I asked Raúl Diego, the sullen, fat-lipped boy to my left.

"I don't know, he fell down the steps. What do I care?"

"Has anyone said how he fell?"

"It was raining. The clumsy bastard slipped. He'll be

back after Easter. What are you, in love with him or something?"

I leaned back in my seat. I breathed, as if from a fresh source of air.

The teacher weaved up and down the aisles as she continued to talk about the Soviet satellite called Sputnik. She said she wished Sergei were in class so that we could get his reaction to the news from his home country. She explained how an object, like the earth or the moon, stays in orbit by falling in such a way that it never reaches what it is falling towards. But mostly she talked about how we were witnessing an incredible time in the history of science, and about how it was important that we remember where we were when it happened, because it was a moment we would want to carry with us for the rest of our lives.

She continued to talk in a high-pitched tone that sounded as much like fear as excitement. And I, still reeling from my narrow escape, had to agree with her: I would always remember this time in my life and that the world that we traveled on was nothing more and nothing less than a thing to be astonished by.

〰〰

The next few days had the breezy lightness to them that comes after a storm has cleared through. By the time Easter vacation arrived, I had put Sergei out of my mind. I gladly got back to my routine of chores and trying to improve myself.

Benita had not come by my house for nearly two weeks. She had been all but ignoring me at school. When my mother told me one day that she had come by looking for me, I knew it had to be because the bottom had fallen out of her friendship with Marisol and Gloria. I decided to make her wait a few days before talking to her. But the next day an even better opportunity for revenge unfolded when I ran into Marisol and Gloria on my way through the Parque Teniente Guerrero.

Instead of pretending not to see them, I cut them off on the path. "I know where you can get cigarettes," I said. "For free. With no trouble."

They looked at each other with raised eyebrows. I turned and they started following me.

At my house I led them down into the basement, where I remembered my father months ago had left two dozen cartons of his favorite cigarettes, Winstons.

The girls squatted down close to the dirt floor, ran their long, thin fingers over the dusty boxes. "What do you want for them?" Marisol said.

"Nothing," I said. "Just let me follow you for a couple of days. Let me spend some time with you. I'll stay out of your way. I just want to see where you spend your time on the beach."

Nothing would get under Benita's skin more than to see me going around with the very people who had dropped her.

Marisol whispered something in Gloria's ear. They looked at each other. They shrugged, nodded. "You can go around with us for a month if we can have all these," she said.

That same day I followed them through the hills towards the shore, where they showed me the hillside crevasse where they spent their hours smoking on weekends and after school.

"Nobody bothers us here," Gloria said. "We can do what we want. It doesn't matter that you've seen it. We move to a different place every few weeks."

It was a cool, overcast day, but they nevertheless flung off their blouses and laid back topless on their blankets, their hair spread out around them in the sand like starbursts. I was speechless with envy at how comfortably they did this, not even looking first to make sure we were alone. I thought they might ask me to do the same, but they never did, and I was glad.

I followed them around for the next few days, trying not to say anything embarrassing. To my surprise, they didn't seem to mind my being there as long as I didn't say anything when we ran into friends of theirs from other schools. I offered to carry their books and blankets for them, and brought leftover tamales from home. And every day on the way home, I made sure we lingered in front of Benita's house for a few minutes before moving on.

One day while we were wading ankle-deep in one of the foamy inlets, the subject of Sergei's accident came up.

"They say that he blinded himself," Gloria said.

"You're an idiot," Marisol said, splashing mud at her calves. "He'll be back in school in four weeks. If he were blind, he would have to go to a blind school."

"You're the idiot," Gloria hissed. "I didn't say I believed it, just that that's what people are saying."

"The fact is," Marisol went on, "that he had an arm amputated. And on top of that, he's suffering from amnesia. He doesn't even know who he is."

"I'm not sure I believe it," Gloria said, but only after a pause long enough to allow the image of a one-armed boy to root itself firmly in our minds.

I knew better than to listen to rumors, especially from these two, but for the rest of the day I couldn't help thinking again about what I had done. I needed the peace of mind of knowing that he wasn't too badly off, and I wasn't going to be able to wait four weeks to get it.

I remembered him telling Profesora Ruiz once that his family lived south of our school in the highest part of the Colonia Obregón. So on the first Monday of Easter vacation I crossed downtown in the direction of the highest hills in Tijuana.

The Calle Segunda twisted and turned up the hill for several miles. The further I rose, the further apart the wood and stucco houses became, with bougainvillea climbing up the sides of some of the porches and lemon and fig trees in the yards. I was getting tired and was about to turn back when I saw a house with a gate sheared off its hinges and overgrown with untrimmed sweet peas. Snapdragons and weeds rocketed up all around the property along a fence that was patched with knobless doors hammered up where planks had fallen away. Through a gap in the fence I saw a pair of patchwork pants swaying from a clothesline. I had found the place.

I didn't go up to the door. I only wanted to get a glimpse of Sergei. But I couldn't see any motion in the house.

I followed the fence down the side of the house to the back-yard gate and peered through the slats. I heaved myself up onto the gate and with great balance quickly walked along the top of the back-yard fence. I pulled myself up into the limbs of a tree in the corner of the yard. I worked my way up into the highest branches for a better view.

Loud chatter spilled from the open windows. Then, after about twenty minutes, the back door sprang open. Sergei hopped out on one foot, his leg in a cast that stretched from toe to thigh. He still had two arms. He carried a dirty yellow crutch, but he hardly relied on it, mostly just dragged it around with him as he clumped about the yard. I waited for him to go back in.

He didn't. Instead, appearing behind him was the largest woman I had ever seen, with shoulders that seemed to strain the seams of her dress and legs even sturdier than mine. Her arms were loaded with cast-iron platters of food and silverware, and a tablecloth was draped over her shoulder. She began to lay a meal out on the grass—right under the tree I was hiding in.

I watched them for several minutes, trying to identify the sweet, meaty smell that was rising from their plates into the tree. After a few minutes I tried to scoot along the limb to get more comfortable, but my skirt caught and I started to lose balance. I reached for a branch. The leaves rustled, sending a shower of blossoms onto the tablecloth they had spread out. They looked up.

I climbed down to the tree's base. His mother jumped to her feet, pulling Sergei close to her as she gasped something in low Russian. But Sergei's face was wrinkled with amusement, as if he had been in on the secret all along. He said something to her in Russian, which seemed to put her at ease. Then, she let out a loud "Ahhhhhhhhhhhh" and gave him a knowing wink.

Excuses were already whirling through my mind when she took me by the arm and handed me her plate. I looked at her.

"She wants you to eat," Sergei said. "Go ahead. There's plenty."

"I was just in the neighborhood," I said, "and I . . ."

She gestured aggressively at the food. I took a mouthful of fried potatoes, and she went into the house for another plate.

"Why didn't you say anything?" I whispered to Sergei. "Why didn't you tell anyone?"

He looked at me in surprise, then limped quickly into the house. I thought I should get out of there while I could, but he came back at once with his hand extended. In it was a cluster of hundred peso bills, the money he had lost in our bet.

"I don't want your dirty money," I said. "Don't you remember what happened? Don't you remember what I did?"

His eyes darted about. I wondered if it was true about the amnesia.

"Look," I said, "people at school were wondering about you, that's all. I thought I'd come and check to make sure you were all right. I'll see you in a couple of weeks."

"I won't be there for a month," he said. He rapped his knuckles proudly on his cast. "I can't climb the hill with this on."

"Oh. Well. Tell your mother thanks." I turned to go.

On my way to the gate his mother caught my arm and gave me a big-toothed smile even broader than Sergei's. "You come back. Tomorrow or after tomorrow. Sergei is by himself. You come back and see him?"

As I let gravity pull me back down the hill, I told myself I had nothing to be scared about anymore. I could stop worrying. Everything was back to normal.

A few days later, as I passed the street that led to Sergei's neighborhood, I thought about how kind Sergei's mother had been, about how earnest her invitation to visit had been. It had been very rude of me to leave without finishing his mother's food or even saying good-bye. I had a bag of a dozen extra tamales that I had planned to heat up over a fire with Marisol and Gloria on the beach. I decided to take them to Sergei's mother instead. I didn't need yet another parent in Tijuana thinking I was unmannered and warning other parents against me. I turned up the hill.

This time I pushed the gate aside and knocked at the front of their house. In the living room, Sergei's mother threw up her hands and came to the door. Her figure was even larger than I had remembered, her enormous shoulders spanning the doorframe and her huge hands pressed flat on her hips. She led me into the living room with much fuss, patting me vigorously on the back as she called up for Sergei.

"I just wanted to drop these off for you," I said, opening my bag. "It's my father's recipe, but I made them."

I looked around the room. From the center of the ceiling hovered an enormous chandelier with many of the glass pieces missing. The room was otherwise spare, but impressive, with a sofa and some throne-like chairs with faded cushions drooping over the sides. Through a door to the right I saw another room that looked just as spacious. In the middle of it, floating in a mist of sunlit dust, was a black lacquer piano.

Sergei must have seen me looking at it when he hopped down the stairs. He took my wrist and led me towards it. I didn't like the idea of him touching me, but I had never known anyone with a chandelier or a piano, and I was curious to see what else they had.

In the piano room I walked around the edges of a dull red carpet, through shafts of warm sunlight, listening to my footsteps echo as if in a museum. At the far side of the room I came to a cabinet filled with plaques and awards. I tried to read the inscriptions, but I had never seen such an alphabet. I was about to ask him to tell me what they said when the room behind me exploded with music. I spun around, holding my breath at the hugeness of the sound. Sergei was sitting at the piano.

He was bent over the keys, leaning into them with the same intensity he showed in school when he was working on a test. The music was unlike anything I had ever heard before. The sound rolled out around him in great swells that swept away all thought. I came closer. His hands seemed to have a life of their own, long fingers dancing vigorously across the keys like angry, but elegant flesh-toned spiders. Then the flood ebbed, pulled into itself as if suddenly embarrassed by its own emotion, and receded to the faintest, saddest trickle of notes I had ever heard.

I stared at his slender back as if he were someone new to me. All at once he spun around on his stool, as if to catch on my face the expression he knew he had produced.

His mother swept in, again carrying plates, this time loaded high with steaming tamales. She set them on a low table by the window that faced the back yard and went out. She left the door open, but not wide open.

My head was racing. "You can play," I said. "And all these awards—they're yours. From Russia?"

He slid his cast under the table and started spearing

tamales with his fork. Through a mouthful of food, he said that his father had also been a musician, a violinist. He had decided to get the family out of the country when the government insisted on separating Sergei from them to study in Moscow. His father's own career had been controlled by such state decisions, and he did not want his son's life manipulated in the same way, no matter how many favors government officials lavished on him. They convinced two longtime friends who were doctors to fake X-rays and test results showing that Sergei was dying from a brain disease that could only be cured in the West. Once he and his mother were out of the country, they went into hiding, first in Switzerland, then in France, taking two years to work their way to Tijuana, Mexico, where many of their relatives had moved twenty years earlier. Only he and his mother had been allowed out. His father was still in Russia.

"Why was it so hard to leave?" I asked.

"My father says that it makes the country look bad when people try to leave," he said. "Besides, they didn't want to lose a national treasure."

I looked at him blankly. It took me a few seconds to realize that he was talking about himself.

As he told me more about what his life as a performer had been like, I stared at him with my fork poised in my right hand. He had been playing piano since he was four and had even met the president of Russia. Electricity traveled in slow waves over my skin. I was sitting in a room with the most fascinating person I had ever met. I was sitting in a room with a genius.

My food was cold by the time I tasted it. "You must really miss your country," I said. "You must miss the attention."

His head popped back in surprise. "This is my country," he said. "And I will be famous no matter where I go."

I jumped up to help his mother clear the plates a few minutes later, but she waved me away. "You come back, play with Sergei? Later this week?"

"Yes," I said, a little breathlessly. "I'll be back tomorrow."

〰〰

When I arrived the next day, I found the two of them in the back yard, trying to lift a stepping stone imbedded in the dirt in order to make room for a new garden.

"Let me help you with that," I called out. I squatted down and wedged my fingers under the stone. I dug in my heels, drove my legs up as hard as I could. In a few seconds it came loose.

Sergei's mother gave a gasp as I hoisted it onto my shoulder and moved it over by the fence. "Don't worry," I said. "I can lift a lot more than this." I got to work on the next stone, then the next. In a few minutes I had moved all fifteen of them.

Sergei applauded me, and his mother patted me on the back. She held me at arm's length. "You are a big girl," she said. "Big and good. Very strong."

It was the first time anyone had ever commented on my size without embarrassing me. As she went back to work in the dirt, I watched the muscles in her back moving under her tight dress. Here was a woman who, it occurred to me now, took large steps when she walked, who laughed and yelled loudly without covering her mouth, and who lifted and hoisted and moved as if these were the things her body was made for. She wore dresses of the most eye-catching green, and never a slimming pleat in any of them. I wondered for a moment if this were some kind of strange dream.

Inside we washed up, and afterwards Sergei played a piece for us that he had just learned, by someone named Tchaikovsky, whose name they made me try to pronounce, laughing all the while at my attempts. He followed this with two sad pieces called sonatas, one by someone named Prokofiev, another by Rachmaninov. Then he closed the lid, refusing to go on, as if he believed that any more would lessen my appreciation of his talent.

I came by after school a couple more times that week, bringing extra tamales and *chicharrones* with me. We lounged in the huge chairs while eating, something my mother would never have let me do. I thought about asking Sergei to give me lessons, but when I looked at the size of my hands, I thought better of it.

Just before the end of the Easter vacation, a strange thing happened. I woke one morning feeling not quite like myself, and yet very much like myself, as if something in the world that had not been right before had suddenly shifted into its proper place. I found that I was no longer resenting things my mother said or mistakes she made or the way she dressed. And when my sister broke my favorite barrette, I had no urge to yell. But most strange of all was the fact that the things I had most been trying to change about myself—my awkwardness, my always getting into fights and arguments—seemed to have fixed themselves. I was lighter in body and mind, as if gravity had released me from the orbit of my old habits. I was flying through life like never before.

I was much more relaxed with Marisol and Gloria, as well. I stopped trying to do things that I thought would please them, and did not hesitate to tell them when I thought they were being nasty and childish. But in spite of their pettiness, I was beginning to enjoy the time I spent with them. They began to take my presence for granted, even came by the house looking for me a couple of times. But I didn't tell them about Sergei. His life carried an aura of secrecy to it that for some reason I felt it was my responsibility to protect.

The morning Sergei was to have his cast off, I was rushing out the back door when I nearly ran into Benita. Her face had the bruised look of a storm cloud waiting to burst.

"Where are you going?" she said.

I stuck my hands in my pockets, leaned casually against the corner of our outhouse. "Nowhere."

"I haven't seen you in a while," she mumbled at the ground.

"Yes, well. I've been busy downtown helping Mamá. And, of course, I've been spending a lot of time with Marisol, and, well, you know . . ." I started to go back in, but Benita loomed close. "They're saying you're in love with the Russian," she said.

I forced out a laugh. "That's crazy. Who told you that? But I'm not interested. Well, it was good to see you." I shut the door.

Through the curtains I watched her disappear. As soon as she was out of sight, I bolted for the Colonia Obregón.

I found Sergei reclined on the sofa with his foot up on a

stack of encyclopedias. "You're not going to believe what people are saying," I said. "They're saying that you and I . . . that we've been . . . that we're sweethearts." The word echoed terribly in the big room. "How could something like this happen? We have to do something."

He smiled at me.

I swirled stormily about the room. "Don't you understand? Don't you see what this means?" Without using his crutch, he hopped to one foot and kissed me.

It was hardly a kiss at all, just a soundless brushing of his lips against mine. But the effect was devastating, like that suspended moment in slipping from a tree or roof when you realize how far you still have to go. Sergei Mikhailovich remembered exactly what I had done to him. But he hadn't cared. Because he had been in love with me all along. And Sergei Mikhailovich was in love with me now.

"I can't stay here," I said. "I never thought anything like this would happen." I was turning to go, when I realized that he was still wearing a cast. I stopped. "I thought you were supposed to get that off today."

I noticed for the first time how pale and tired he looked. "The bones didn't heal right," he said. "The doctor had to reset them."

"You mean . . ." I swallowed.

"They had to re-break the bones," he said weakly.

"What about school?" I said. "You can't afford to fall further behind."

He shrugged, as if that meant nothing to him, then sat down again. I stood for a long time, not knowing what to say. His eyes fluttered with exhaustion. After a few minutes, he drifted off to sleep.

I made sure to meet Marisol and Gloria at the river on time the next day. I didn't care what they thought about me and Sergei, but they were the hub through which all gossip passed. They could demolish a rumor as easily as give life to one. The day was hot, and in rolled-up pants we settled down by the shore. They didn't mention Sergei, but their curiosity hovered in the air with the persistence of summer insects. Then, as we were talking about how Rico Candelario had disfigured his face playing with gunpowder, Marisol casually lobbed the first grenade.

"Even so, he still isn't as ugly as, let's say, Sergei Mikhailovich."

I could almost hear their eyes click towards me in their sockets.

"I agree," Gloria said. "Or as dirty. They say he never bathes."

I gave them no reaction.

"You wouldn't know anything about that, would you, Margarita?"

I yawned, stretched my limbs out in the sun. "Actually," I said, "I've been to his house a few times."

They lifted their heads slightly off their blankets.

"Oh, yes," I said. "His mother buys tamales from my mother. But she has a bad back, so I often deliver directly to their house. She often invites me in. Did you know they have a beautiful piano?"

Their heads settled down again, the rumor dead.

When I got home, Sergei was waiting for me, crutch in hand, on the front steps. In the late afternoon shade, his face shone pale with discomfort. It was nearly two miles from his house to mine.

"What are you doing here?" There was no harshness in my voice.

"Why haven't you come to see me?" he said.

Never before had he looked so thin, and his eyes were ringed with dark circles. He tried to say something else, but trembled on his crutch as if about to collapse. I reached out for him and caught him, eased him back onto the steps. When he had his strength back, I walked him home, stopping so that he could rest along the way. At his front door, he leaned against me. He smelled of cinnamon and chocolate. There was nothing dirty about him.

When I went by to check on him the next day at noon, he was looking brighter, nestled into the big sofa in the living room. He offered to play the piano for me, but I wouldn't let him get up. Instead he told me more about his plans to someday be a composer. That would come in time, I said. First, he had to recuperate so he could get back to school.

Over the next few weeks, we slipped back into our habit of seeing each other. I stopped spending time with Marisol and Gloria. His mother asked if I would mind helping her with the garden one or two days a week until Sergei was better. She wanted to start planting zinnias, she said, though it was long past the season for planting zinnias. I told her I would be more than happy to.

The rumors, of course, began to grow again. I could see it in the smirks of the kids I passed on the street in my neighborhood, in the fact that Marisol and Gloria stopped coming by my house looking for me. But in the comfort and warmth of Sergei's music-filled house these things seemed far away. I let myself sink into whatever each day presented.

One night, after spending nearly the entire day at Sergei's house, I lay in bed thinking about what I had fallen into. I had made so much progress in finding ways not to stand out, and now I was once again going to be the center of jokes and attention. Unable to sleep, I rose before dawn and made my way to Sergei's house.

It was still dark when I got there, and there was no movement in the house. I climbed the fence to the back and knocked on the glass. He came to the window rubbing his eyes, his hair in a tousle.

"Get dressed," I said. "You're coming with me."

He met me in the street out front in rumpled clothes, his crutch tucked under his arm. I started leading him down the hill just as the sun was coming up. He looked at me, as if shaking himself out of a dream.

"Where are we going?"

"You don't want to miss any more school, do you?"

It took us an hour and a half to get to the school. Most of the students had already arrived. The morning air was cool and very still. We approached the steps of the school. My heart was beating hard, but I ignored it. I knew what I had to do.

A few people sitting at the bottom of the steps were the first to notice us. Then other heads started turning our way. A younger boy, probably a fourth- or fifth-grader, elbowed his friend in the ribs. There was no turning back. I slid my arm around Sergei's back. I lifted him up into my arms and started to carry him up the steps.

Everywhere people began to point. I kept climbing. Behind us someone let out a long pig-like squeal of laughter. I tried to keep my eyes focused just a few steps ahead of me.

The climb seemed like it would never end, as if I were scaling an escalator that was going backwards. I passed Benita, frozen with a look of astonishment. And from above, like two horrible predatory birds, Gloria and Marisol grinned down upon us.

They parted for us at the top without a word. I set Sergei down and together we walked to Profesora Ruiz's class to tell her that Sergei would be starting school again.

The rest of that day was full of whispered talk and laughter. I could feel people watching me, but I didn't look back. I told myself that as long as Sergei could keep smiling, I could bear it as well.

Every day for the rest of the school year, I met Sergei at the bottom of the hill before school and carried him to the top. And every day we endured jeers and taunts. I started getting into fights again, but Profesora Ruiz didn't try to punish me with extra assignments or make me stay after school. She did scold me privately after class, but the softness of her eyes told me she was on my side.

Sergei and I went back to our old schedule of late afternoons at his house. One day it occurred to me that there was no reason for him to always be confined to his house. I decided to take him to the beach where Marisol and Gloria and I used to meet. So on the first day of summer, I carried him down the steep slope to the shore. It was there that he admitted to me that he had started the rumors about us. He had been downtown and had seen Raúl Diego from our class and had told him everything about the time we had been spending together. I widened my eyes in pretend shock. I took his crutch and started to walk away as if to abandon him there for his crime.

"Margarita!" he called out. "Come back! Please! I'm sorry!"

I ran back to him, sweeping him up into my arms until we were both exhausted with laughter. He said my name over and over, his sandpapery Russian accent smoothing away the harshness of the consonants of a name I had always hated. We promised each other that as soon as our parents would allow it, we would marry, and we talked of how we would travel around the world attending his concerts and lectures. We would have a beautiful home that would always be full of music. And, when I was ready, he would even teach me to play. Every day the world around us shifted a little more, making room for new possibilities.

The letter from my father telling my mother to bring us to the United States came on the tenth day of summer. I was walking through the door, having just returned from taking Sergei to the Parque Teniente Guerrero, when my mother's glowing face told me everything I needed to know. We were to leave at once, she said, bringing only the clothes we needed. Papá would come back to Tijuana with one of my cousins to take care of selling our things and transferring ownership of the house to my mother's sister.

"Margarita is right," he wrote. "There is no reason for us to be apart any longer."

I had only enough time to see Sergei twice before we left. As I climbed the hill to his house, I felt a dull throbbing in my head. I went in without knocking and found him at the piano, running his fingers up and down the keys, releasing a spirited string of notes. I stood watching him for a long time, not knowing how to interrupt him, or what I would say. When he finally noticed me, he jumped up with his crutch and hobbled over to greet me, smiling as always.

It took me a long time to force the words out. I told him I would come back with my father in a few weeks to see him. I would be able to come back many times each year, especially if our new business did as well as my father was hoping. I said we would hardly have a chance to miss each other.

Sergei had little to say, but kept his smile up throughout. After all, he said, his concerts would someday bring him to the United States. In the meantime, we would write every day and keep in touch. There was no reason why we shouldn't someday fulfill our plans.

He turned back to the piano as I said good-bye. Leaving the house, I heard the same tune he had been playing when I had walked in. But now the notes were much slower, and further down the scale. It wasn't the same song at all.

That night, as my mother and I began to pack, I searched my belongings for something to give Sergei, something he could carry with him to remind him of me until I came back. But I could find nothing that was valuable to me, nothing that I thought would interest him.

In the closet I shared with my sister I found a container of red nail polish that I had once bought without my mother's permission and hidden in a shoebox. I took it with me the next morning when I went to see Sergei for the last time. With it, I painted my initials on his cast.

"You should just be getting this off by the time I come back," I said with a cheerfulness I had learned from him.

"I wish I had something for you," he said, and for the first time I could see the sadness seeping into his face like blue ink spreading through water.

I told him that it didn't matter. I told him I had everything I needed to remember him.

During my first week in Sacramento I wrote Sergei daily, sometimes even twice a day, telling him all the details of my new life. My father promised me that in time I would start to forget him, that the pain would become bearable. In the meantime, he said, it would help if I focused on making new friends and adjusting to my new surroundings. Here, he told me, was a chance for me to make a fresh start with my life, just as he and Mamá were doing with theirs.

I got to work at once helping with the new business, boxing and loading the tamales that my uncle's wife made onto a truck behind his huge, gleaming kitchen. At night Tío Ramón gave me English lessons, which I picked up quickly. By the time summer was nearly over, I was speaking well enough to get by and had even made friends with a couple of girls who would be in my same class.

Over the next few months, life in Sacramento turned out not to be as wonderful as my father had said it would be, nor as bleak as Benita had foretold.

It has now been four years since I last saw Sergei. Getting along with people here is no easier or more difficult than it was in Tijuana. The business has kept us all too busy to return to Tijuana as I had hoped we would. It will probably be a long time before I see the ocean again, but there is a river here. I like to go there on weekends, though sometimes this means going there by myself.

As my father predicted, I began little by little to forget Sergei. Today I can honestly say that I no longer miss him. But that does not mean that he is no longer with me, or that our story has come to an end; for because of him, every day I am left with the feeling that I am falling through my life rather than living it. I am falling, not the way that Sergei once fell, but the way I had once been told that the earth in its orbit is forever falling towards the sun, falling into it and soaring above it at the same time, always soaring and falling, falling and soaring.

Jesús Colón

Jesús Colón was born into a poor working-class family in Cayey, Puerto Rico, in 1901. Colón's daily exposure to strong-minded ideals led him to develop a type of philosophy similar to socialism. In 1917, he immigrated to Brooklyn in search of a new life, and soon became familiar with the abuse and exploitation of the working lower class. He experienced discrimination when he was denied an editorial position because he was not white. This reality greatly impacted Colón, moving him to write about the Puerto Rican working class in the United States. He started a newspaper for Spanish-speakers, and eventually landed a position as a columnist at the *Daily Worker*, a New York-based Communist-party newspaper. Colón defended Latino workers, speaking against the injustices they suffered daily. His political activism led him to run for public office with the Communist party in 1969, and during his time at the *Daily Worker*, he was president of Hispanic Publishers. His volume of essays, *A Puerto Rican in New York and Other Sketches* (1961); his autobiographical accounts, *The Way It Was and Other Writings* (1993); and the only recorded Spanish-language collection of his chronicles, *Lo que el pueblo dice* (2001), all recount the challenges faced by the Puerto Rican workers in New York. Colón's politically active nature is apparent in his writing, ardently portraying the will of the immigrant worker who fought to survive in a new world, facing not only economic hardships, but also the discrimination that, in the end, made the Puerto Rican worker stronger.

He Couldn't Guess My Name

Coney Island is not what it used to be. The old Coney of Luna Park and Steeplechase are gone forever. So is the "parachute jump," where you were thrown head first from a suspended parachute down to the ground. You were then given time to gather your pen and pencils, small diary book, letters and papers, which, snatched by the wheel and the pressure of the fall, had flown from your pockets.

On one of my visits to Coney Island during the "good old days," I was attracted by a crowd responding to a man who, while mingling with everybody, was putting questions to individuals in the group.

"What's your name? Just murmur your name in my ear," the man was saying. Then he printed the given name on a large white card and held it up for people to see. He then asked his blindfolded partner, standing on the platform, what was the name he had printed on the white large card. Invariably and instantly the blindfolded man answered: "The name is Mary." "The name is Peter." "The name is John."

Then the man, still walking among the crowd, came to me and asked the customary question: "What's your name?"

"My name is Jesús," I answered in a familiar tone of voice.

"What did you say your name was?"

"My name is Jesús."

"Again?"

"My name is Jesús Colón."

He printed my name on the usual white large card and showed it to everybody.

I showed him my library card, social security card, and personal letters to certify that my name was indeed Jesús.

With the names John, Mary, and Peter the man walking among the crowd just threw the coded phrase words pertaining to those familiar names to his blindfolded partner on the high platform. And—eureka!—the answer was flashed back to the audience in a matter of seconds. But this time, when he asked my name, a long dialogue back and forth between the blindfolded man and the questioner amused the whole group. The question man was hemming and hawing. His previous rapidity and fluidity of language had been replaced by tongue-tied monosyllables almost inaudible to the rest of those present. The question man was sweating profusely.

When all the rephrasing of the words shouted to the blindfolded man failed to elicit my name from his stuttering lips, the questioner came to me with a "prize." Take this prize and get the hell out of here.

Imagine sending Jesus to hell!

I kept the prize with me for many years. It was a tiny plaster of Paris copy of Rodin's *The Thinker.*

I kept it with me as a reminder that man, as yet, doesn't know everything.

Beatriz de la Garza

Beatriz de la Garza was born in the town of Revilla, now called Ciudad Guerrero, Tamaulipas, Mexico. In 1952, at eight years of age she moved with her family to Laredo, Texas. In Laredo, de la Garza attended school and began to learn English. At that time, she began writing in Spanish, and as she learned English, began to write in her new language as well. In high school, de la Garza dedicated herself to writing fiction, and was given honorable mention two consecutive years by *Seventeen Magazine* for her short stories. She studied journalism and creative writing at the University of Texas, where she also received an M.A. and a Ph.D. in Spanish. She then received a law degree from the University of Texas School of Law. As an undergraduate, de la Garza won a short story contest sponsored by the student literary magazine *Corral*. *The Candy Vendor's Boy and Other Stories* (1994) and *Pillars of Gold and Silver* (1997) portray de la Garza's beloved hometown, depicting the magic of the Mexican culture to readers. De la Garza has served as president of the Board of Trustees of the Austin Independent School District, and is currently a practicing attorney and writer. Her most recent book, *A Law for the Lion: A Tale of Crime and Injustice in the Borderlands,* came out in 2003.

Pillars of Gold and Silver

The thought comes to Stella that afternoon that perhaps she dislikes the child. "Nonsense," she tells herself, "I am a teacher. I like children. I am a teacher because I like children." On their own, though, her steps slow down as she approaches the classroom where he waits for her. She looks at him through the window, sitting in a miniature chair. He is too big for the kindergarten furniture and yet too small for his age. No child should look like that, she thinks, noticing the resigned angle of the shoulders, the hopelessness of the hands in his lap.

They go through the hour-long drill, as they have done for the last month, almost every afternoon of the school week. "This is a pencil," holding up a pencil. "This is a pen. Pencil—*lápiz*. Book—*libro*. I open a window," as she walks to the window and tugs with it. "*La ventana*—the window." She uses the flash cards; she acts out verbs. "What is your name? *¿Cómo te llamas*? My name is Paul. *Me llamo Pablo*. I am Paul. *Yo soy Pablo*."

She repeats the phrases, usually first in English, then in her slow, careful Spanish. The child sits silently, an apologetic expression on his face, as if he were sorry to be troubling her this way. He regrets that she has to stay late after school just for him. He is even a little embarrassed for her as she exaggerates the actions that she is illustrating: "I open the door. I sit down. I stand up." Throughout it all he

122

remains in his island of silence. He wants no part of this activity on his behalf.

He had been this way ever since his arrival, some three months ago, his aunt said, when she brought him to school. He might as well not speak any language. His aunt looked middle-aged, although she could not have been more than thirty-five. He was nine, very close to ten, she thought. The parents were dead. A violent death such as seemed endemic south of the border, from the Rio Grande to Patagonia. Death from revolution or political repression, crime or undifferentiated violence—it all amounted to the same, Stella had thought as she sat through the interview with Pablo's guardian, translating between the aunt and the school principal.

The hour-lesson is over, and she tells him it is time to go. This, being Friday, she also wishes him a good weekend. She speaks to him in English, hoping to trick him into revealing that he has understood her, but he does not move. His body stiffens in the ignominiously small chair, but he remains still, like an animal that has been trapped before and now does not trust his instincts. She repeats the dismissal in Spanish, and this time he gets up and walks out of the room with that odd gait of his that is almost a shuffle.

She leans back in her chair and closes her eyes. Does the child have a speech impediment, after all? Does he have a learning disability, the term now favored over retardation? She knows that, in the past, children who did not speak English were labeled as retarded due to lack of speech development in a foreign language. But that happened in the dark ages, before schools became enlightened to the needs of the foreign children who had begun appearing at the school doors. How had they done it before, when the waves of Slavs and Italians were arriving at Ellis Island? They had somehow learned English. I did it, after all, she thinks, as she stands up briskly and begins collecting her handbag and her notebook.

♒

It was the summer of nineteen-fifty-something. Fifty-two or fifty-three, somewhere around the time when people began wearing buttons that said "I Like Ike," that the men came to the little house and brought a little box with medals and ribbons in it. They gave the box to the young woman, but it did not make her happy. She looked at the medals, and she began to cry. Other people came, too, and embraced the beautiful young woman, and sometimes they all cried. Sometimes they would also remember the little girl and give her hugs, too. The little girl would often hide in the kitchen when the people came. She hated to see them cry, and she was frightened when she heard the grown-ups weeping.

One day the young woman and the little girl packed their suitcases and got on a bus. They left behind them the emerald lawns and the flower boxes, the sea that roared just out of hearing and the blue mountains in the distance, and rode into the heat and the grays and browns of the desert. They rode for several days as sweat trickled down their backs and their thin dresses clung to their seats. They would stop sometimes and get out to stretch their legs under the blazing sun or to go eat sandwiches in dim little stores that smelled of coffee and spices. They rode over mountains and past landscapes pocked with craters and dunes and over hills and across little streams. The little girl slept a great deal of the time.

Then they got out again, and this time their suitcases were unloaded. It was very hot. The little girl had never felt heat like that. It was like standing in front of the oven when you opened it to take out cookies. Her mother was talking to a fat woman inside the little store that also had gasoline pumps outside. There was a bench just outside the door, and the little girl sat down to wait for her mother to come out. She could hear her talking inside. They were talking in Spanish. She knew it was Spanish because that was what her mother spoke to her at home. Nobody else around them did. The little girl understood what her mother said to her, but she wanted to talk like June and Linda, who were her best friends from next door. They spoke English and so did their mother. *Her* own mother would also speak English when they went shopping or when she talked to the neighbors. She spoke it funny, though, and said some things wrong, but she was such a pretty and sweet young woman that nobody minded much, and they all thought it was cute the way she talked.

The man by the gasoline pumps was calling to the people inside the store that the car was coming, and her mother and the fat woman came out. Her mother asked her if she needed to go to the bathroom and hurried her into the little cubicle inside. Her mother knew the driver, and they talked as they loaded the suitcases in the trunk. Her mother rode in the front seat with him, and the little girl had the back seat to herself. The leather seat cover was cracked, and the springs sagged as they drove away. After a while they turned off the paved road and took a dirt track.

The little girl looked back, but all she could see was the cloud of dust that they trailed behind. Suddenly there was a hanging bridge ahead of them. She became terrified when she saw it swaying in the wind and realized that they were going to cross it. Her mother did not seem worried, though, and continued talking to the driver. The girl looked down and saw a sullen, brown river, slithering over large, flat rocks between the sandy banks. Then they were across the river, and two men in khaki uniforms stopped the car and talked to the driver and to her mother. She saw her mother laugh for the first time in a long time. The men waved them on.

She saw something white shimmering in the distance. The driver, who was a big, gray-haired man with a brown face, turned to speak to the little girl in the back seat and, pointing ahead with one hand, said, "That's Revilla just ahead." She nodded politely. It did not mean anything to her.

They drove down a long, dusty street lined with houses made of stone, whose walls rose like cliffs directly from the street. Some of the houses were whitewashed, and the glare from the sun which they reflected dazzled her eyes. Others had exposed sandstone blocks where the stucco had peeled off and had a mottled look, like an animal shedding its fur. They had massive wooden doors that sometimes stood half-open and door-length windows protected by iron bars. Nothing stirred in the noonday sun—only a few dogs that huddled close to the walls, looking vainly for shade. She could hear no sound save a chorus of cicadas and the cooing of turtledoves in the distance.

They stopped before one of the mottled houses, and the driver honked his horn. A plump, gray-haired woman wearing a black-and-white print dress came out wiping her hands on a white apron. The little girl remembered that her mother had been wearing nothing but black for some time now. The two women embraced for a long time, and then both began to cry. The little girl leaned back against a corner in the back seat. She did not want to see crying again. Suddenly, the older woman was opening the back door of the car and lifting her out in her arms, kissing her and clasping her against her. The little girl looked at her mother, the question in her eyes.

"It's your grandmother, *tontita*. You silly little thing!"

"What did you expect, Lilia? I haven't seen the child since she was in diapers. I would have known her, anyway. She gets her eyes from Roberto. She takes more after her father's family."

They were standing in a covered entryway that opened into a dusty courtyard—a *patio*, as she came to learn that it was called. Flower pots lined the whitewashed walls of the entrance, and the floor was made of rough paving stones. In the middle of the courtyard stood a stone structure, which her grandmother soon identified to her as the cistern from which they took all their water and into which— under no circumstances—was she to try to peer into it. A metal bucket with an attached rope rested upside-down next to the cistern.

It was dinner time, and they had a delicious broth made with beef and cabbage and corn and squash and onions and tomatoes, and they had hot corn tortillas, which they shredded and dropped into the soup. It was the first hot meal they had in days, and it made the little girl sleepy. The grandmother set up a narrow canvas cot in front of an open window and told her to go to sleep. She fell asleep to the murmur of the two women's voices in the next room.

They now lived in this new place where everything was so old. The strangeness of their new life did not overwhelm her as it could have though. She took her cue from her mother. Her mother accepted that lights did not come on at night anymore by flicking a switch, and so did she. Instead, they lighted a kerosene lamp when the sun went down, and if the lamplight threw gigantic shadows against the wall and never reached the far corners of the rooms where the portraits of ancestors brooded in the gloom, this did not frighten her, because her mother was not afraid. Going to the outhouse *did* scare her, but her mother would go with her and stand by until she conquered her fear.

Other things were even fun, such as taking a bath in a galvanized tin tub in the kitchen while her mother poured bucketfuls of cold water over her, or sleeping outdoors at night. If it was hot, they would set up canvas cots in the courtyard, secure behind the high walls that surrounded them and the massive doors with their iron bolts. Lying in her cot, the little girl would look up at the sky and ask her mother about the stars above. In the morning, the sun would wake them up as it came over the walls that enclosed the courtyard and dry out the sheets that had become damp with dew during the night.

In the mornings, the two women cleaned house and then cooked the main meal, which was at noon. In the afternoons they sat in the cane-backed rocking chairs and sewed or knit while they talked of relatives that the little girl had never met. While they talked, she would look at sepia-tinted photographs pasted in albums or gaze at her parents' wedding portrait. Her mother looked very much the same

as in the picture, just a little thinner now, and was very pretty in her white wedding dress. She gazed intently into her
father's eyes, seeking to find in them her own, those that
her grandmother had said she had.

She had no recollection of him, just a shadowy memory, more like a dream, of his strong arms holding her high
up in the air and then setting her down on his shoulders
while he pretended to gallop like a horse. She heard the two
women recount the story of her parents' courtship. She
heard how Roberto would come across that swaying bridge
every Sunday, rain or shine, cold or hot, to promenade with
Lilia around the plaza while her brothers stood by the
bandstand in the middle of the square and maintained their
vigilant watch in place of their dead father. She was their
only sister, and they were going to make sure that no one
trifled with her.

The brothers had since married and left to make a living in the city. They now urged their mother to come and
join them where she could be close to them and enjoy the
conveniences of modern city life, but she refused to leave
her house. She knew she wanted to die and be buried next
to her husband, close to friends and neighbors. She did not
want to lie, after death, among strangers, when all her life
she had lived among friends.

The older woman would then urge her daughter to come
back, if not to live with her, at least to live close by, among
her dead husband's family, across the river. But the young
woman would become agitated and say that there was no
future down there, on either side of the river, in either country, and, besides, she had never gotten along with Roberto's
mother and sisters.

The little girl was a habitually quiet child, but she was even more so now. She did not want to offend her grandmother by speaking to her in a language that she did not understand, but neither did she feel up to addressing her in Spanish. She communicated indirectly, therefore. She would whisper what she wanted, in English, to her mother, who would then translate. Finally, the older woman exploded in irritation: "Lilia, if you don't do something, this child is going to end up mute! I don't know how much English she knows, but I know that you do not know much of it yourself; and she does not know Spanish. We have to teach her. She has grown up like a plant without roots, like those plants that hang in the air and attach themselves to whatever they find. Give her roots! Teach her what she is and who she is."

After that, her mother encouraged her to say things directly to her grandmother, and she did because she did not want to make her angry. Her vocabulary was getting better from listening to the two women talk every day, and her grandmother seemed pleased. What she would not do was go out to play with the children from the neighborhood. Every evening, after supper and after the sun had gone down, the children would come out to play in the street. They would hold their games in front of any of several houses within a two-block range, and sometimes they played directly in front of her grandmother's house. The little girl would watch them from the embrasure of the window, refusing her grandmother's encouragement to go out and join them. The games involved songs, chants, and riddles, linguistic feats that she was not willing to attempt for fear of their ridicule. One evening a little boy, who was the youngest in the large family that lived next door, came to the window and asked her to join them, but she merely shook her head and withdrew hastily from the window. She enjoyed watching them, though, and gradually came to recognize several of the tunes of their games and even learned some of the words.

One day came a shattering blow. Her mother began putting her clothes in her suitcase, and the little girl, thinking their visit was at an end, began to do the same. Her mother stopped what she was doing and, taking her aside, explained that she was going away by herself. Just for a little while, she hastened to add, as she saw the look of horror on her daughter's face. "Estela," she always called her just "Estela," and not "Blanca Estela," as her grandmother did. "Estelita," her mother said, "I am going away for a little while. I have to look for a job to support us. You will stay with your grandmother until I find a job. It will be just for the summer, just for a little while. She will take good care of you, and you will be company for her. She is lonely. And then I will come back for you, and you will start school in English. It will be like we had planned to do— before your father went away." Then she began to weep, but she dried her tears quickly. "Do you remember your father?" How could she tell her about the memory of being held by those strong arms, of the hard muscles under the starched fabric of his shirt when he would hold her up in the air, about the thrill of those gallops on his shoulders? She had probably dreamed it. "You were such a baby when he left," her mother continued. "He went to war, you know, and they killed him there. He was very brave. That was why they brought me those medals, but I don't want the medals. I want him." The little girl ran out of the room, and when she came back, her mother finished packing.

Early the next morning the car, which must have been one of only four or five in town, stopped in front of the house. The little girl stood rigidly in front of the massive doors of the *zaguán* as her mother climbed in the front seat with the driver. Only after the car had driven off and her mother had stopped waving back at them did she give in to the overwhelming need to run after it, but her grandmother stopped her just as she was breaking away and held her tightly against her. She tried to push away this hateful old woman that smelled of sun-dried clothes and soap. Estela finally escaped her and hid in the only hiding place afforded by the open, rambling house. She went in the outhouse and latched herself in and only came out when it got too hot inside.

Then it was as if she had finally reached the mute stage that her grandmother had predicted. She would not speak. Her grandmother did not force her to talk either, but spoke to her as though she expected no response. She would ask her to fetch water from the cistern and give her careful instructions so she would not fall in. She would give her a small sack of beans to clean before cooking them. She would ask her to find a particular button in the box with the boating illustration on the lid. She would have her thread a needle for her. In turn, she seemed to guess the little girl's wants and needs. She knew that the little girl disliked the taste of boiled milk, so she would disguise it in frothy, cin-namon-flavored chocolate that she whipped with a wooden whisk. She would brush her hair at night until it soothed her and made her sleepy. In the long afternoons she would read stories and fairy tales to her from a stack of books that always sat on a table in the parlor.

But the grief of abandonment stayed with her. One night she woke up sobbing out of a dream that she could not remember. She only remembered how sad it was. Her grandmother took her in her arms and sat her in her lap and rocked her in the cane-backed chair while she sang to her the lullaby of Saint Anne—the lullaby that Saint Anne had sung to her grandchild, the baby Jesus.

A letter came from her mother on the following day, and the grandmother read it for both of them because the little girl did not yet know how to read. She was not six yet.

That evening Estela left the shelter of the window and stood out on the sidewalk while the children played. The little boy, whose name was Fernando, came to ask her again to join them and even taught her the words to the game they were playing. Under a full moon she sang and joined hands with them as they chanted rhymes of games whose counterparts she later learned in another school and another language. They were all barefooted, and she still remembers to this day the feeling of the cool, gritty sand as it burrowed into the crevices between her toes. When it was time to go to bed, her grandmother washed her feet and kissed her good night.

From then on she joined the children in their games every night until the mothers came to the doorstep, if they were inside, or took in their chairs, if they were sitting in the *zaguanes* or on the sidewalk, and called them in to go to bed. And later, in the morning, she would hear the rumble of the big truck that came to pick up the children to go to the fields to pick cotton. Many earned spending money this way, and she had wanted to join them there, also. Fernando had even offered to teach her how to hold the burlap sack and fill it with cotton bolls, but her grandmother had refused her permission to go with them. "You are not used to being out in this hot weather in the middle of the day. You might get sunstroke." And so they left without her, but in the evenings she would be waiting for them.

One game that they played was *Doña Blanca.* The children formed two concentric circles while they held hands, and a child stood in the center of both. She was Doña Blanca, the Lady Blanche. She was a princess shut up in a tower. The children in the outer circle marched in one direction while they sang about the Lady Blanche, who was surrounded by pillars of gold and silver. They would break down a pillar to see the Lady Blanche, they sang, as they tried to break in past the inner circle. Sometimes the arms of the guardians of the inner circle held fast, but sometimes a weak link would be found, and the rescuers would stream in to rescue Lady Blanche. Doña Blanca was the favored child, the Queen of the May. It was never the little girl, but she did not hold it against them. It would have embarrassed her to be singled out.

One day, again at noon, the car brought her mother back. The little girl was ecstatic. She had so much to tell her. She chattered—in Spanish—to her mother about the games and the other children and about how they went picking cotton and earned money doing so, and how Fernando, the little boy next door, her best friend, was going to start school in September, and she wanted to go to school, too. Her mother was pleased with her, but she also seemed pleased about something else. Her face was not as pale as before, and her eyes were brighter. She was now wearing a black skirt with a white blouse, instead of the black dresses that she had worn before. Late that night, the little girl could hear the two women talking, sitting in the dark before an open window, while she lay in her cot in the courtyard.

The next morning her mother told her that she had come to take her back with her. She had found a job. It was factory work and did not pay much, but, put together with her widow's pension, they could manage. She, her darling Estelita, would start school in September—in English— and she would make new friends. "But I was going to go to school with Fernando," was her only response. Her mother explained again. She would go to school in English, on the other side. "Will June and Linda be there, too?" she wanted to know. No, they were going to live in another town. There would be new friends. A vague apprehension settled over her, coupled with a feeling of importance. She told the other children that night that she would soon be leaving to go to school "across the river, far away—in English."

The evening before they left, she was chosen to be Doña Blanca. As she stood in the center of the two circles, she felt happy. The children on the outer circle wanted to reach her and be her rescuers; the ones on the inside wanted to keep her for themselves. They sang: *Doña Blanca está encerrada / en pilares de oro y plata. / Romperemos un pilar / para ver a Doña Blanca.* It did not matter who won. What mattered was that they wanted her.

The next day she kissed her grandmother good-bye and promised to write to her very, very soon, as soon as she learned how to. She promised to come back next summer.

She promised Fernando that she would go picking cotton with him next year. And as they drove away, she clasped in her lap the precious button box with the most precious buttons in it—her grandmother's farewell gift.

On the return journey, men in green uniforms stopped them on the far side of the bridge. These men did not smile or make conversation with her mother. They merely looked at the papers that she showed them and asked her many questions, first in broken Spanish and then in English, until she became irritated and had to bite her lip to control her temper. Finally, they waved them on without a smile.

Then there was a new town and a new home—a small apartment where there was not much light and little room to move in. There was school, too, for the first time. It was a school where they only spoke one language, the language that she had almost forgotten, and which did not have words for many things. There were friends, eventually, to play with on the playground, but none to play with by the moonlight. She was never again the Lady Blanche.

Then came Poppy, her stepfather, and a new family. Her grandmother died soon after the twins were born, and none of them went to the funeral.

ᨆ

And I never went back. She died, and she is buried now among her friends, next to her husband. Who tends those graves now? Perhaps the uncles who are now strangers forever, perhaps the cousins that I never met. Perhaps now Estela hears the call of voices from across the years and across the miles and knows that things always return to their beginnings. But I never went back. Not the following summer to pick cotton with Fernando. Not ever. I turned my face away from them all, away from that world that I came to be ashamed of, ashamed not only of it because it seemed so foreign, but ashamed of myself, too, for having once been happy there. I never went back. And now I do not know where I belong.

≈
≈

She puts away the notebook with her writings and goes back to bed. When she wakes up, it is evening, and she bathes and prepares dinner in an effort to regain some semblance of a normal schedule, but her head feels dull and aches. The following day is Sunday, and she follows her usual routine for the day, preparing lessons and readying her clothes for the week ahead. She even finishes hemming up the skirt that she had left undone. She does not look again at what she has written.

Monday, after school, she finds Pablito in his usual place. She is about to begin the scheduled lesson when she changes her mind. She reaches out to him and takes his hand, pulling him out of the too-small chair. She leads him out to the playground and to the swings. She sits him in a swing and then takes another one herself. They sit in silence for some time, swinging gently as she looks around the school yard. The school grounds are lovely, a green rolling field bordered by a small stream. A far cry from her own school with its all concrete play-slab and chain-link fence enclosure. A far cry from the sandy street, lime-white in the moonlight.

She begins to hum and then to sing softly the words from the games of long ago, which come to her unbidden.

There is *Doña Blanca* and *Naranja dulce*, where the beloved is compared to a sweet orange, a song of farewell. Then there is *Hilitos de oro*, about the spinner of golden threads who refused the king his daughters. She thinks—now, as an adult—that the games that children learned when she was a child, and perhaps still learn today, must be of medieval origins. They were about knights saying farewell to their ladies as they left for wars or about rescuing the fair Lady Blanche. Each game acted out a story, a song. Their music had reached her once, long ago; perhaps the music will reach Pablito now.

She stands up and pulls Pablito out of his swing in one motion. She takes his hands again and begins walking in a circle while she sings about rescuing Doña Blanca. Pablito looks at her in bewilderment and then begins to laugh. She laughs with him. When she can stop laughing, she says to him: "*Yo soy Doña Blanca. Me llamo Blanca. Blanca Estela.*"

Pablito nods his head, a knowing smile on his face. He makes a mocking bow: "*Yo soy Pablo.* My name is Paul."

Sandra María Esteves

One of the founders of the Nuyorican poetry movement, Sandra María Esteves is a "Puerto Rican-Dominican-Borinqueña-Quisqueyana-Taino-African-American," born and raised in the Bronx. Growing up in a culture whose language of English and Spanish intermixed, she was not allowed to speak Spanish in school lest she be punished. That is when Esteves turned to art to express herself, and continued doing so until adulthood. While studying fine art, she began associating with writers, and soon discovered that she had a talent for writing herself, transposing the emotions portrayed with colors and shapes into the art of the written word. Esteves has written several poetry collections, among them *Bluestown Mockingbird Mambo* (1990), and *Yerba Buena* (1981), which received recognition from the *Library Journal* as Best Small Press. Esteves has received international recognition and awards, including the Arts Review 2001 Honoree from the Bronx Council on the Arts and the Edgar Allan Poe Literary Award in 1992 from the Bronx Historical Society. Her poetry has been published in several anthologies, magazines, and literary journals. Living in New York, Esteves continues creating art, writing poems, and teaching workshops, as well as collaborating in spoken word productions.

Religious Instructions For Young Casualties

Believe in yourself.
Be all that you can.
Look for your fate among the stars.
Imagine you are your best when being yourself
the best way you can.

Believe in yourself. Be all you want to be.
Open your mind, a window to the world,
different ways of thinking, seeing,
but be yourself—it's the best.

Become your dreams, visions to live by.
No matter what anyone says,
believe you can do it.
Day by day, a little at a time.
Be patient.

Believe you can find a way
to assemble the puzzle called life,
forming pictures that make some kind of sense.
Even when pieces fall scattered to the ground,
disappearing into the finite void,
forever lost, never to be found,
choosing your future from those that are left,
like one piece from some other dimension.

Maybe a corner triangle shape of sky,
or zigzag of ocean floor with seaweed and one school of fish,
or maybe a centerpiece on the table in some fancy dining
     room,
or patch of window lace curtain next to flowered bouquet,
wind blowing through sunlight, which some artist will
     paint someday.
Or bouncing feet on the moon,
walking in giant moon leaps, talking moon talk,
deep into research in your flying laboratory.

Be all that you can, but believe in yourself.
Climb the stairway of your imagination, one baby step after
     another.
Growing like the leaf, blossoming into a great tree,
complete with squirrels, nests, universe all around.

Be all that you can,
just believe in yourself.

Affirmations #3, Take Off Your Mask

Study the face behind it.
The one that has no flesh or bones.
The one that feels what the universe feels.

Take off the mask. Discard it.
Useless shell that it is.
An old skin. A cover.
Subject to weather distortions.

See for yourself
the you inside no one else can see.

♒

Life Is A Journey

. . . on a greyhound bus
arriving at your destination
like a young girl, self-conscious,
worried about her looks.

At the station the bus pulls up.
Waiting in line are her ancestors
wearing blue and white ritual clothes,
their faces long and serious.

She thinks she has to get new clothes.

Virgil Suárez

Born in Havana, Cuba, in 1962, Virgil Suárez knew he wanted to write at the young age of twelve. Suárez was forced into exile with his parents in 1974, and moved to the United States. Then and now, he writes to remember his experiences in exile, putting into the written word his pain, anguish, fears, and passion. Suárez studied creative writing at California State University at Long Beach, where he received his B.A. and then graduated from Louisiana State University in Baton Rouge with an M.F.A. in Creative Writing and Contemporary American literature. His writing has been published in numerous literary journals. Suárez's work includes *Infinite Refuge* (2002), *The Cutter* (1998), *Spared Angola: Memories of a Cuban-American Childhood* (1997), and *Welcome to the Oasis and Other Stories* (1992). He has also co-edited various anthologies, including the first anthology of Cuban-American literature *Little Havana Blues: A Cuban-American Literature Anthology* (1996) and the best-selling anthology *Iguana Dreams: New Latino Fiction* (1993). He won the 2002 G. MacArthur Poetry Prize and a 2001–2002 National Endowment of the Arts in Poetry. Suárez is a professor of creative writing and Latino/a literature at Florida State University in Tallahassee, where he lives with his family.

Ricardito

Manuel and Josefina's only son. Like me. We both lived in an imagined world. We played together. He was a couple of years older. A bit slow. As old as he was, he drooled, and spittle always collected in the corners of his mouth, a frothy gob. We sat by the side of the house and scared each other with ghost stories. While we told stories, we played with the mud-turned-clay in his mother's garden, which wasn't a garden at all but a strip of earth between the house wall and the fence. There, coffee plants grew, and it was here where we made clay soldiers and we fought wars, and because he was older, he always won. One day, and this my mother still claims, I got so mad at him that I filled my milk bottle with urine, then I told Ricardito that it was orange juice and, being thirsty, he drank it. I don't remember this story, but my mother says it is true. Josefina and Manuel, she says, had a good laugh. They were always doing that, it seemed, laughing at their one and only son. My mother, whenever she needed to give me a shot, took me over to Ricardito's where she proceeded to bend me over her knees and then inject whatever it was that I needed. Those, too, were the days that both Ricardito and I were always taking something that was supposed to be "so good" for our health. Our mothers gave us Scott's Cod Liver Emulsion, all kinds of vitamins, *jarabes* for growth and stamina. Funny how none of it helped in terms of the distance and the different lives Ricardito and I have lived. He, still in Cuba; I, in the United States. He, finding his own mother dead in her bedroom three days after she had died of a heart attack. All the time, the tetracycline our mothers took during pregnancy was turning our teeth yellow-green. I also have a lasting image of him on the day I learned how to ride my bicycle without its training wheels. As I took off, he ran after me, in the clumsy way children with orthopedic boots do, shouting, "*¡Dale, Dale, Dale!*" Still today, as my own daughter learns to pedal her bike, I cannot help but run after her, shouting, "*¡Dale, Dale!*" and I think of Ricardito still in Cuba.

Daniel Chacón

The last of three children, Daniel Chacón is a Californian by birth. He received a B.A. in political science and an M.A. in English from California State University at Fresno. He received his M.F.A. from the University of Oregon. Even before graduating, Chacón was writing about life as a Chicano living among different cultures, incorporating into his work his own experiences as part of the Mexican-American community. In *Chicano Chicanery* (2000), Chacón's characters often find themselves struggling to fit in an environment completely foreign to them. Some finally adjust, yet others clash with their new realities and with the people around them. Chacón has written several other short stories and essays published in more than half a dozen literary journals. He has also written several plays produced in Oregon and California. While writing, Chacón taught English for five years at Modesto Junior College, California, and for one year he taught creative writing at Southwest State University, Marshall, Minnesota. Chacón is currently working on literary projects and teaching fiction writing and translation in the English Department at the University of Texas at El Paso.

Too White

Ifelt bad for the kid but wanted to laugh at the fat cop, who looked around the scene with his eyes squinted as if he were the greatest detective. His fat cheeks and the front teeth that touched his lower lip made him look like a little kid with a badge and a gun. That afternoon I was alone, having gone in the grocery store to walk the tall aisles of wine and liquor, hoping to have guts enough to stuff a bottle down my baggy pants to share later with my friends Johnny de la Rosa, David Romero, and Gilbert Sanchez, who were, like me, among the few Chicanos in our town. Usually we walked the Livermore streets together, feeling like giants, strutting past small homes that seemed barely to reach our waists, thinking we were bad. We weren't a gang, but we had thought about giving ourselves a name. Kids our age avoided us.

The crowd was pressed so close that our shoulders touched. Suddenly some kid on a ten-speed bike broke through to the front. His handlebars were raised up like ram's horns. He stopped and rested his elbows on the chrome bars, and his face in the palms of his hands.

"Damn," he said, blue eyes wide. "What happened here?" He looked at me, expecting me to answer.

"Some kid got hit," I said.

"Friend of yours?" he asked.

"Nope."

The poor kid, sobbing softly, his bike mangled out of shape, lay in a fetal position on the asphalt.

"Damn," he said. "I'm glad it wasn't me."

From across the parking lot the ambulance wailed as it swerved its way through shoppers quickly pushing carts to their cars, and it came to a stop at the scene. The paramedics jumped out, lay the boy on a stretcher, and took him away. The kid on the bike and I were still standing after most people had left, and he was staring at the blood spots where the boy had lain. This kid was my age and had very short hair and so many pimples on his face that his skin was red and purple. He wore braces, too, the kind that needed to be strapped around his head. An ugly kid. Uncool.

The fat cop approached us. "All right, boys," he said, flipping the page of his note pad and licking the tip of his pen. "What did you see?"

I turned away because I didn't like cops.

"We didn't see anything," the kid said.

"When did you boys get here?" he said, pressing pen to pad, as if we would provide the clue he needed.

"Just a little while ago," the kid said and turned to me. "Isn't that right?"

"Yeah, that's right," I said. "We didn't see nothing."

He flipped his pad closed, looked us up and down, and said, "You boys stay out of trouble."

"Asshole," I said as he waddled away.

The kid laughed. "Hey," he said to me, "you want to go to my house?"

I didn't even know his name, had never seen him before.

"Sure," I said, "let's go."

The house seemed empty, our voices echoing off the beamed ceilings. The sliding-glass doors to the back yard looked out onto a sparkling pool, which was the shape of the number eight, a diving board, and a flower garden with blues, reds, and greens. I felt like I was in a movie.

I followed him down the hallway into his bedroom where he had his own pinball machine, only slightly smaller than the pool hall kind, and a stereo system better than the one my family shared. On his walls hung posters of football stars and rock bands whose names I didn't know.

But it was what he had on the bedside table that caused me to pause: money, a few dollar bills and lots of quarters, dimes, and nickels. I looked at the money, then at him, but his head was under the bed, because he was trying to pull something out. I pictured myself putting the money in my pocket and running out of there, but not just yet.

I didn't even know his name.

He piled a bunch of thin boxes on his bed, Monopoly, Parcheesi, Life, and he said, "You want to play?"

I stayed all afternoon playing Monopoly. When I landed on Park Place, which he not only owned but had placed a hotel on, he jumped off the bed and started dancing, rolling his arms as if he were swimming, then holding his nose, covering his mouth, and sinking deeper into water. "Oh yeah!" he yelled before he shook his head, face blurring. When he stopped, his eyes bulged and he said, "I'm the greatest."

That made me laugh.

After he had left his room to get us stuff to eat and drink, I looked at the money on the table. It shined and yelled for me to take it. I had none in my pocket, and no prospects of getting any.

He came back with his arms filled with bags of chips, Hostess cupcakes and Twinkies, cold cans of Coke, and assorted candies. He threw them on the bed and said, "Take whatever you want."

"Wow. This is like 7-11," I said. "My mom never buys this stuff."

He shoved potato chips into his mouth, his face raised to the ceiling while he laughed. As he was still chewing, he looked at me and said with crumbs flying out of his mouth, "I hope you didn't steal any money while I was gone."

"What the hell you mean by that?" I said.

"I'm winning," he said. "So if suddenly you come out with a hundred thousand dollars and buy all kinds of hotels, I'll be suspicious."

I laughed. "You're okay," I said.

"No, I'm the greatest!" He threw the bag of chips on the bed, stood up and moved his arms back and forth like an Egyptian. "The greatest! The greatest!"

I giggled. "What's your name, anyway?" I said.

"That's right. We don't even know that," he said. "I'm Kenny."

"I'm Joey," I said.

"Hey, you like music?"

"Yeah, what do you have?"

"Everything," he said. He jumped from the bed and opened his closet, revealing stacks of record albums as high as our knees.

"Do you have Tower of Power?" I asked.

"Never heard of them," he said.

I named off several other bands that Chicanos like me and my friends listened to—Mary Wells; Earth, Wind and Fire; The Isley Brothers, but each name seemed to leave him more confused. Music could divide, could tell us who we were, who we weren't.

He was too dorky, too uncool. Too white. No one could know about this day. I would deny it ever happened. I looked at the money on the table.

"You decide," I said.

He pulled out an album. "This is my favorite," he said. African-sounding drums beat furiously, and then there were screams and wails. We continued playing while Mick Jagger crooned,

Please allow me to introduce myself

Kenny moved his head to the rhythm of the music as he held the dice in his hand, shaking them like a spiritual rattle, blowing on them for luck.

Pleased to meet you
hope you guess my name

Damn it, I couldn't help it: I liked this kid.

That evening I walked home along shadows of tall trees, past homes with vast lawns, down an avenue lined by a brick wall beyond which were more rich homes, onto another avenue dotted with duplexes and small, sagging houses, past Johnny de La Rosa's place. One of his older brothers was working on a car, a naked bulb hanging from the hood, swaying slightly, glowing like a halo. I reached my street—cars on blocks, scrawny, misshapen trees—and went into my home, into my life, where my father, smoking a cigarette, sat shirtless on the couch, stomach flab hanging over his waist. He was watching a boxing match. My mom, at the tiny table in the kitchen, sat before a sewing machine, the whir of the needle a soft sound like an electric razor. "I'm home," I announced. They looked at me like I was crazy. As if to say, "And?"

During lunch, we Chicanos hung out at the far end of the field, next to the chain-link fence that separated school grounds from the tall wooden fences of people's back yards, me, Johnny de la Rosa, who had long black hair in an Indian braid and wore a red bandanna, David Romero, and Gilbert Sanchez. We were too cool to be involved in anything that went on in junior high, too cool for junior high.

About fifty feet away, a group of white girls sat in a circle smoking cigarettes. They kept looking back at us.

"Would you ever do a white girl?" David Romero said to anyone. David we called Romeo because he always wore slacks, shiny shoes, and his hair was slicked back.

Adrian, a little dark kid who wasn't cool but liked hanging out with us, said, "I know I wouldn't. No way. How about you, Johnny? Would you? How about you, Joey?"

I took a drag off my cigarette, too cool to answer.

"You don't like girls," David said to Adrian. "So shut the hell up."

"That ain't true. I like girls."

"Yeah, your mama," said Johnny.

"I wouldn't," said Gilbert Sanchez, the only one of us sitting down, his arms straight in back of him. Gilbert was skinny and he wore glasses, and he seemed from a distance to be a little geeky, but up close, you could see that his arms were long and thick with muscles and his face was solid as if chiseled from stone. "I wouldn't want no white girl," he said. His teeth were yellow and crooked.

"I don't know if I would or not," said David Romero. To him the question mattered, because he liked a pretty blonde in our class named Naomi and he wanted our approval to pursue her. "What about you, Joey?" he asked me.

"That's probably all he likes," said Gilbert.

What other options were there? I thought. The Mexican girls in our school were traditional Catholic girls who wouldn't even kiss, or else they were Gilbert's sisters, but nobody was stupid enough to try anything with them.

I looked over at the girls in the circle. "Hell yeah, I would. If she was fine."

"Shit yeah," said Johnny, and he raised his hand to me for the Chicano shake.

"Yeah, me, too," said Adrian. "If she was fine."

"Shut up, boy," I said to him. "Why don't you go get us something to eat or something? What did your mama give you for lunch?"

He lifted a brown bag from the ground and looked inside. "I got burritos and some chips."

Gilbert looked at me, cocked his head, squinted his eyes, and said, *"Quieres casarte con una gabacha, ¿eh?"*

"Well, uh," I said. "You know . . ."

He slowly shook his head, looking at me. *"No me entiendes, o ¿qué? ¿No eres mexicano?"*

"Let's go talk to those girls," Johnny said to me.

I watched Gilbert, wondering what he was thinking. His small black eyes quivered behind the glare of his eyeglasses. He had a scar on his chin, as if he had been cut with a knife. Suddenly he perked up, seeing beyond me. "What the hell?" he said.

From the school buildings, where kids played on the blacktop or on monkey bars, a white kid was walking toward us. I knew it was Kenny by the sparkle of his braces in the sun.

"If he comes over here. I'm going to kick his ass," said Gilbert, who was tall and fast and knew karate. He was the best fighter in our group and the one who enjoyed it the most, like dancing he had once said, rhythmic and measured. "I'll kick that white boy's ass," he said.

Kenny got closer, but he stopped and craned his head to get a better look. He was looking for me.

Johnny, fingering his long hair around an ear, said to Adrian, "Friend of yours?"

"That geek? Hell no," said Adrian. "I ain't got no friends like that."

Kenny stood still for a while, and then he turned around, and walked away.

"Boy's lucky," said Gilbert.

Johnny and I went and talked to the white girls.

His mother was a tall, beautiful blonde who looked so elegant picking blue and red flowers from their garden that I was unable to look her in the eyes when Kenny introduced us. "He's a seventh-grader like me," he said, which made me feel small and young, not the way I wanted her to see me.

She stood up, a bouquet in her gloved hands. "Welcome, Joey," she said, and when she smiled at me, I wasn't sure it was the way an adult smiles at a child, but rather the way a woman smiles at a man. She wore navy-blue sneakers and tight nylon pants rolled up at the ankles.

"Kenny, make sure you take out the garbage this afternoon. Tomorrow's garbage day."

"Shit, man!" he said. "I always got to do the slave work around here."

"Just do it," she said, bending over to pick up her hand shovel.

"You do it," he said as she walked away. "I ain't a slave."

"Am *not*," she said.

That afternoon we swam, we played pool on the table they had in the family room, and then we ate sandwiches his mother made, on a long wooden table that shined so much we could see ourselves in the reflection, our faces distorted and cartoonish like in a funhouse mirror. Kenny pulled his mouth wide with his fingers and stuck out his tongue and the mirror image made him look so goofy that I spit milk from my mouth laughing.

I was too embarrassed to have him see my house, so I went to his place a lot, almost every day, telling my friends that my parents were cracking down, keeping me at home a lot. On weekends his family would do things together. His dad was a lawyer, a thin man who was nice to me and who didn't smoke or cuss or lift his hand to Kenny and tell him to shut the hell up. If anyone did any cursing, it was Kenny, right in front of his parents, and it shocked me that they didn't do a thing about it.

One weekend I went with Kenny's family to the mountains and stayed in a cabin. Kenny and I pretended we were thieves running through the woods with a million dollars in a duffel bag, chased by the police. A bear trap snapped my foot, practically cutting through to the ankle. "I can't keep going," I cried. "Leave me here to die. The money's yours."

"No, we're in this together," he proclaimed. "What's the point of being rich if I can't share it with my very best friend?"

The trees of the forest glittered with sun.

I stood up, suddenly serious, suddenly angry.

"What's wrong?" he said.

My very best friend.

"This is a stupid game," I said.

"It's fun," he said.

"I need a cigarette," I said.

"You don't smoke," he said.

I looked at him standing there, his arms out as if asking why.

He was such a dork.

He was so white.

Too white.

I could see the veins in his neck.

Suddenly we heard rock music coming from beyond a cluster of trees, and we froze. Then, with question marks in our eyes, we looked at each other. Kenny motioned me to follow, and like spies we pushed our way through thickets. In a clearing next to the lake was a Winnebago, and sitting outside of it were two girls, older than us, about sixteen. They sat on lawn chairs in bikinis, one holding a tanning device on her chest like a giant book of mirrors.

"Damn," said Kenny. "Girls."

"Yup," I said. "Them's girls."

"You like girls?" he asked.

"What kind of question is that?"

"Just wondering," he said. "Some guys don't. Some guys think they have cooties."

"You mean kids," I said.

"Yeah, kids, like us."

"I ain't no kid," I said. "I like girls."

One of them, a brunette with her hair in a ponytail, stood up from her chair.

"Damn," he said.

We heard the bell his parents sounded for dinner, so we ran through the woods, the branches of trees and bushes swatting me on the arms and face.

Inside the cabin, we sat around the table, the father, wearing a cardigan sweater, and the mother, in a tight pink blouse with a V-neck, on one side and Kenny and I on the other. There was a plate of hamburger patties with melted cheese, a plate of buns, and another with chopped lettuce and tomatoes. "Dig in, boys," said the father, and Kenny grabbed a bun and put two patties on it. Around his parents I was shy and timid, so I sat there waiting until his mother looked at me with her sky-blue eyes and said, "Go on, Joey. We barbecued them."

"Thank you," I said; and slowly, shyly, I reached for a bun and placed it on my plate. Then I reached for a patty. Kenny started eating, holding his burger to his mouth and chewing happily.

"You kids having fun today?" the father asked.

"We're going swimming after we eat," said Kenny.

"We have to wait," I said. "An hour after we eat or we'll get cramps."

"That's just a myth, Joey," she said. "You can swim whenever you want."

"But my mom said you'll get cramps if you don't wait."

"It's just not true," she said.

The father interrupted: "What does your dad do for a living, Joey?"

"Oh, he's a, he works for the nuclear lab," I said.

"Is he an engineer?" she asked.

"Well, he does, I'm not sure exactly." He was a janitor there. "This hamburger looks great," I said, looking at it sitting on my plate.

"Don't you want lettuce and tomato?" she asked, lifting the plate from the table.

"Oh, no thanks. I just like meat."

"Have you ever been to Disney World?" the father asked.

"You mean Disneyland?" I asked.

"No, I mean Disney World. In Florida."

"I've never been out of California," I said.

"No way! Really? Gosh, I've been everywhere," Kenny said.

"Last year we went to Europe," she said.

"That was boring," Kenny said.

"It was not. You had a great time," she said.

"Well," said the father, smiling and looking at me and Kenny. "We're going to Florida this summer. To Disney World."

"All right!" said Kenny. "It's about time."

"He's been asking us forever," she said to me, and only

to me, as if we had a private moment. The hamburger on my plate looked so good.

"Here, Joey," she said, in almost a whisper, her long, thin fingers taking hold of my bun, opening the burger, exposing the meat. Gently she laid another patty on top. It looked stacked, abundant. "If you like meat, you should have two patties. A double burger," she said. Then she slid the bun back on. I couldn't wait to bite.

"Thanks," I sheepishly said.

"We'll spend three days at the Disney hotel," the father said.

"Wow, that's neat," I said. "You guys should have fun."

"Would you like to come with us?" the father asked, and then he and she looked at each other and smiled. Then at me. "We know you're Kenny's best friend, and we think he'd have a lot more fun if you were there."

She winked at me.

"You got to come," Kenny said.

"Well, I don't think we can afford it. I mean, I have brothers and sisters and . . ."

"Oh, you won't have to pay anything," she said. "Kenny would have a lot more fun if you were there."

"I sure would," he said. "In fact, I ain't going without you."

"Kenny," she said, as if he had said something wrong.

Obediently, he said, "I am *not* going without you."

"What do you say?" the father said. "You want to come?"

"Uh, yeah, sure."

"Well, then," she said. "I'll call your mommy and get the permission. I look forward to meeting her."

Mommy?

The plate was dark brown, like blood.

"We'll be flying there," said the father.

"On a plane?" I asked.

She laughed, her silver necklace reflecting. "Yes, Joey, on a plane."

"I never been on a plane before."

"This is so cool," said Kenny. Then he turned to me. "Best friends forever," he said, raising his hand for a high five.

His parents were watching, smiling, the father placing his arm around her shoulder. They looked as if they had just done something wonderful and could see the reflection of it in my relationship with their son. My face felt red. I lifted my brown hand. "Forever," I said, feeling the sting of his slap against my palm. They laughed, and everyone started eating again. Except for me. The hamburger looked too big, too much.

"Eat, Joey," she said. "Please eat."

After school, we Chicanos and some white girls were at the park across the street from campus. One girl hung on Johnny and another one was holding on to my arm. Her name was Melody. She looked around as if she thought she were bad, daring anyone who passed the park to look at us. She wore jeans and a halter-top. Gilbert sat on a picnic bench, without a girl, and David on another bench, sweet-talking Naomi.

Johnny said to his girl, "Tell me what people say about me."

"You're baaad," she said.

"What else?"

"Hey, man, when are we going to start our *clika?*" Gilbert said.

"Let's do it," said Johnny.

"What's a *clika?*" Melody asked me. She was a pretty girl with a tiny nose and blonde hair.

"That means gang," I said.

"You guys are going to start a gang?" she said.

"Why not?" said Johnny.

"I think that's cool," said Johnny's girl.

"You do?" I asked.

"I'm going to Fresno next week, *ese,* and I got a cousin who's an F14. He could give us some pointers," said Gilbert. "All members have to get jumped in. I know that much."

"What's that?" asked Johnny's girl.

"We all beat the hell out of each new member," he answered. "It's fun."

"What are you going to call yourselves?" asked Melody.

Johnny, in a slow Chicano drawl, nodding his head, as if it were the coolest-sounding name ever, said, "The Locos."

"That's a stupid name," said Gilbert. "How about Los Killers?"

We all seemed to notice at once some pale kid on a bike pedaling toward us. My heart jumped because I saw that it was Kenny. Gilbert stood up. I had once seen him throw some guy on the ground and kick him repeatedly in the head. He had a violent streak like none of us had. We just liked being bad, the image, but Gilbert liked hurting people. "I just thought of a requirement for the gang," he said. "Kill a white boy."

Kenny stopped his bike in front of us, rested his elbows on the raised handlebars. "Hey, what's happening, fellas?" Then he looked at the girls. "And ladies."

The girls looked at us as if they didn't think he should have the right to be in our presence.

Too slow, too casual, Gilbert walked over. He was going to fly a kick to Kenny's head. Kenny said, "Hi, Joey, you want to go to my house?"

Gilbert looked at me, scandalized, but with a slight smile that said he wasn't really surprised, that he had almost expected it. "This guy's your friend," he said. "This white boy's your buddy."

"Hell no, he ain't," I said. "Get out of here, you little piece of shit," I said to Kenny, stepping between him and Gilbert.

"I got him, Joey," Gilbert called, as if Kenny were a fly ball.

"This one's mine," I said. "Get lost, white boy."

"Bullshit," said Gilbert, "I saw him first."

"What?" Kenny said. He couldn't believe it, didn't recognize me.

"Get out of here," I said, and I pushed him so hard in the chest that his bike fell over and so did he, sprawled on the sidewalk. We all laughed, David, the girls, Johnny, all except for Gilbert, whom I stepped in front of because he was getting ready to kick Kenny.

"Get out of here, you wuss," I told Kenny. In the tone of my voice I heard that I was warning him, protecting him, but that wasn't how it sounded to him.

When he got on his bike, he was crying, not because of pain, at least not physical pain. "Get out of here before I kill you!" I yelled. I bit my lip.

He stumbled on his bike and rode away. "To hell with you," he cried. And then he said it again, but in a scream so painful it sounded as if he were falling off a cliff.

To hell with you!

He rode to the end of the park, heading for the exit. His eyes must have been blurry because he crashed into a picnic bench, flying off his bike and landing on the asphalt. We heard the thump. Sobbing. I knew he hurt. He hurt bad.

"Hey, man, what the hell did you do that for?" Gilbert said, stepping up to me. "That white boy was mine."

"Get out of my face," I said, looking Gilbert in the eyes like I was ready to fight.

"You better not be challenging me, punk," he said, stepping in closer.

"Go to hell," I said. "I'll mess you up."

"What did you say?" he whispered, raising his arm, biceps rising, cupping his hand to his ear. "I didn't hear. What did you say?" He came even closer. He pointed at his ear. "I must be deaf or something. I didn't hear what you said."

"I said I'll mess you up."

"That's what I thought," he said, slowly nodding, and then in a blur of speed his fist came at me. I tried to block but it was too fast, and it hit me on the eye like a baseball bat. My eye shut.

I wildly punched back, but all I felt was air.

"Punk," he said over and over as he hit me on the side of the head and on the mouth. "You fight like a white boy," he said.

Blood dripped down my lips. I hurt, but I kept fighting, kept missing, hoping, as Gilbert kept hitting, that Kenny was watching.

Gilbert stopped, as if I had enough. With his arm, he wiped some sweat from his forehead. "You ain't good enough to be in our *clika,* man. You're too white."

"You punk," I yelled, lunging at him. I grabbed him around the shoulders and pulled him close. I could smell his cologne, his sweat, and for a moment he did nothing, just accepted my embrace, breathed hard, his warm breath on my neck. We moved around in each other's arms, stepping sideways like exhausted boxers, slowly hitting each other in the ear, the side of the head, the mouth.

I pushed him away and punched him hard on the mouth. His glasses fell off, and he looked down at them stunned, surprised. He looked cross-eyed, like a geeky little kid. I hit him again, so hard my fist hurt. He came after me, but I sent two to his face, both of them connecting, causing him to stumble back, and then I sent two more to his chest and ribs.

When he bent over, I lunged at him, but he deflected me aside and kicked me in the back of the head, his boot like metal. I fell to the ground, and before I could get up, I felt shadows surround me. Through blurry eyes, I saw three figures standing over me. Then I felt the kicks all over my body, and I heard laughter. Then a siren. The cops were coming. They were all beating me, David, Johnny, Gilbert. I was the first to be jumped in.

Victor Villaseñor

Victor Villaseñor was born in the barrio of Carlsbad, California, on May 11, 1940. He grew up on a ranch a short distance from Carlsbad, in Oceanside, in a house without books and where only Spanish was spoken. Starting school, Villaseñor spoke no English, and because of this language barrier and his dyslexia (which he did not know he had until years later), he eventually dropped out of high school. Frustrated and ashamed of being a Chicano, Villaseñor gave college a try, but again had to drop out, still having a hard time with his studying. He decided to go live in Mexico, and it was there, at the age of twenty, that he read Homer's *Odyssey*. It was also in Mexico that Villaseñor learned to take pride in his language and his heritage. He returned to the United States ready to defend his identity as a Mexican, and while reading James Joyce's *Portrait of the Artist as a Young Man*, decided that the best way to defend and to educate people about the value of his cultural heritage was through writing. For ten years Villaseñor wrote nine novels, and 65 short stories, worked as a construction worker, and received 265 rejections before finally selling his first novel, *Macho!* (1973), which was immediately compared to John Steinbeck's best work. Since then, Villaseñor has written an award-winning screenplay, "The Ballad of Gregorio Cortez," the national best-selling nonfiction drama *Rain of Gold* (1991), later published in its Spanish edition, *Lluvia de Oro* (1996), and the collection of young adult stories *Walking Stars: Stories of Magic and Power* (1994). Villaseñor lives and writes in his childhood ranch home in Oceanview with his own family.

Toreando el tren
or
Bullfighting the Train

In the next few days, Juan met many boys his own age as they waited alongside the railroad tracks. There were boys from all over the Republic of Mexico, and they were on their way north to the United States with their families, escaping the Mexican Revolution.

A few of the boys liked to gamble, so Juan set up foot races with them to see who was the fastest, and they threw rocks to see who was the strongest. And Juan, who was eleven and had always thought he was pretty strong and fast, lost most of the contests.

Many of these boys were really powerful, especially the full-blooded Tarascan Indians from the state of Michoacán. In fact, Juan figured that some of them were probably as good as his long-legged brother, Domingo, who'd been five years older than him and one of the fastest and strongest boys in all their region of Los Altos de Jalisco.

Domingo and Juan had been closest in age, and they had been raised together. Juan missed Domingo dearly. He'd disappeared just two months before they'd left their beloved mountains. But their mother still thought that there was a good chance that maybe Domingo was alive and hadn't been killed, like all his other older brothers.

Juan and his newly found friends played up and down the

tracks and through the burned-out buildings, pretending to be Pancho Villa and Emiliano Zapata and other heroes of the Mexican Revolution. They were mostly nine, ten, and eleven years old, and they just couldn't wait for the day when they would be big enough so they, too, could take up arms.

Juan told the boys of the different incidents of war that he'd seen up in his mountainous region of Los Altos, and how brave and courageous his brothers and uncles had been.

Hearing Juan's stories, the other boys told their stories, too, and little by little Juan grew to understand that either these boys were huge liars or in other parts of Mexico they'd truly had it much worse than his family had it up in their isolated mountains.

Not until the last year had the war really hit them up in Los Altos de Jalisco. Before that, José, Juan's greatest brother, and a handful of local boys had managed to keep their mountains free of war, just as Don Pío and his rural police had managed to keep them free of bandit gangs years before.

"*¡Miren!*" yelled Juan, hitting his legs with a stick. "I'm the famous Four-White-Stockings stallion of my brother's! And here come five hundred horsemen after me, but I jump across the *barranca*, and they all fall to their death!"

"Me, too!" said another boy named Eduardo. "I'm the great Villa! And here I come to help you, Juan, with my Dorados del Norte—the finest horsemen on the earth!"

"Oh, no, they're not!" said a third boy, named Cucho. "General Obregón's cavalry led by Colonel Castro are the finest!"

"Hey, that's my cousin!" said Juan excitedly. "On my mother's side! My great uncle Agustín's fifth son!"

"But I thought you were for Villa!" said Eduardo. He was almost twelve and the strongest of them all.

"I am!" said Juan. "But I'm also for my cousin! How can I not be, eh?"

The boys played and challenged each other, throwing stones and racing. Then it was the day for Juan and his family to go north. They got on the train along with the thousands of other people, getting in one of the tall empty cattle cars. But the floor of the car was so full of cow manure that they had to get back out and shovel all the *caca* out by hand before they could find a place to sit down for the long ride north.

But, they had no more settled in and the train started moving, when Juan got up and sneaked out of the boxcar along with five of his new friends.

The day before, Juan, Eduardo, Cucho, and three other boys had made a bet among themselves to see who was the bravest of them all. The bet was to see who would stay alongside the tracks as the train took off and be the last one to run and jump on the train.

They called this *toreando* the train, or bullfighting the train, and all six boys realized that this was a very risky game because, if they didn't catch the train and they got separated from their families, it could be for life.

Juan's heart was pounding with fear as he now stood alongside the tracks and watched the huge iron wheels of the train turning slowly in front of him, carrying the long row of cars down the tracks. He watched the train weighted down with people, stuffed full in the boxcars, piled high with their bags and boxes on the flatbeds. His heart went wild, but still he held and he watched people holding on every which way they could so they could get to the safety of the North. Juan was full of the devil; he just knew this was one event.

After all, he was a Villaseñor with Castro blood, and all week long these boys had been outdoing him in throwing rocks and running foot races. But now he would show them in one great, swift challenge what he was truly made of. For he, Juan, was the boy who'd gotten a man's reputation up in his mountainous region at the age of six when he'd proved himself to be so brave that it was said that his blood ran backwards from his heart.

Oh, he would never forget that night. It had been a full moon and the local witch had put a curse on his family. So it was up to the youngest, who was purest of heart, to redeem *la familia*. And he'd done it.

Licking his lips, Juan glanced at his friends as the train started moving a little faster. He felt like a bantam rooster. After all, he had the blood of his grandfather, Don Pío, running through his veins.

"Getting scared, eh?" said Eduardo to Juan as the train slipped past them. He was the oldest and strongest of them all and the second-fastest runner.

"Not me," said Juan.

"Nor I," said Cucho.

The big iron wheels were turning faster, crying metal to metal as the long line of boxcars and flatbeds went by. Five thousand people were going out that day, and there wouldn't be another empty train going north for weeks.

Juan's heart began to pound. Oh, how he wished these boys would just get scared and run for the train so he, too, could run after his family.

The huge iron wheels turned faster and faster. A part of Juan's mind started telling him to stop this ridiculous game and jump forward and get on the train to join his mother while he still had the chance. But he wouldn't move. No, he just held there alongside the other boys, refusing to be the first one to give in.

The sounds of the big turning, sliding, moving iron wheels on the shiny-smooth steel rails were getting louder and louder. The huge long train—well over fifty units and two locomotives—was picking up speed. Finally, one of the younger boys couldn't stand it anymore, and he screamed out.

"I'm going!" He leaped forward, catching one of the passing boxcars and swung on.

"He wants his *mamá*!" laughed the boys.

Juan and the other boys laughed at him, saying that he was a cowardly little baby.

Why, the end of the train hadn't even slid by them yet, so they ridiculed this boy. But still, down deep inside their souls they all knew that he'd done the right thing and they all wanted to be with their *mamás*, too.

Then came the end of the train, coming by them at a good pace, but still not going so fast that a good runner couldn't catch it. Juan grinned, feeling good. Now it truly took guts not to cry out and run. So there went the end of the train, cranking iron to iron past Juan's face. It left him and all the other boys behind, going up the long, desolate valley. A second boy now cried out in fear.

"This is stupid!" he screamed. "We could lose our families forever!"

He took off running after the end of the train and swung

on. Once more Juan and the boys who'd remained behind laughed, calling this other boy a coward, too.

"Well, I guess this only leaves us, the real *hombres!*" said Juan, watching the train beginning to pick up speed as it went up the long, flat valley.

"Yeah, I guess so," said Cucho, "but at least I'm the fastest runner, so I can afford to wait. I don't know what you other slowpokes are doing here. It's four days by horseback to the next town."

And saying this, he suddenly took off running up the track. He, Cucho, the fastest boy among them. Juan wanted to scream out in fear, but he didn't. He held strong. He had to. He was from Los Altos de Jalisco, after all.

"Darn Cucho," said Eduardo, who'd been left behind with Juan and another boy, "trying to scare us. Heck, a good man can always outwalk any train. All you need is water."

"Right," said Juan, trying to act like he, too, wasn't scared. But inside he was ready to pee in his pants, he was so terrified. "With water, a good man can always survive," he added.

Juan held there alongside the two tall, lanky Indian boys, but it was hard. Juan was beginning to lose the power inside himself. He wasn't one of the fastest runners, after all. And the train was getting farther down the tracks.

Then another boy took off. He was tall and fast, but, still, he was having an awful time catching the train. He held on to his hat, running as fast as he could, arms swinging, bare feet lifting, and got up close to the end of the going train. But he just couldn't get a hold.

Juan glanced at Eduardo next to him.

"Hey," he said, "we even outwaited Cucho, the fastest of all, so I think we've shown our worth!"

"Yeah, let's go!"

"Yeah!" said Juan. "We both won!"

So they both took off down the tracks and, in the distance, the last boy finally got hold of the train. He tried to swing up, but he lost his footing and his legs almost went under the steel wheels.

Seeing this, Juan screamed out in terror and ran with all his might, arms pumping, feet climbing, having run up and down mountains all his life. He ran and ran, gaining on the train, but the pace was killing him.

But then the front end of the long train hit a small downward grade. Suddenly, the whole train jerked forward, picking up speed. Eduardo gave it all he had, pulling ahead of Juan.

Juan saw the train going, and he thought of his mother and his sister. He could imagine the grief and terror in his mother's old face when she discovered that he wasn't on the train and she'd lost yet another child. Tears came to his eyes, and he got more scared than he'd ever been in all his life.

"*¡Mamá! ¡Mamá!*" he cried out in anguish.

He raced on with all his heart and soul. The people on top of the boxcars looked back and saw the two boys running after them. But they thought they were only local boys playing, so they just waved.

Gripped with the sudden understanding that he'd lost his mother forever, Juan lost all hope, and he tripped, falling face first into the sharp rocks between railroad ties and ripped open his mouth.

He lay there spitting blood and choking, and his eyes

flowed with tears. The tall, lanky Indian, who'd gotten a good fifteen yards ahead of him, came walking back slowly.

The long train was gone now. It was a good quarter of a mile down the tracks, whistling and picking up more and more speed as it went north from the city of León toward Aguascalientes, Zacatecas, and Gómez Palacio, where it was supposed to stop over for the night and refuel before going on to Chihuahua and then Ciudad Juárez across the Rio Grande from El Paso, Texas, in the United States.

Coming back, Eduardo saw that Juan was all bloody, and he offered him his hand.

"Well," said Juan, getting to his feet and wiping the blood from his face, "let's go! We've got to catch that train!"

"Don't be crazy, *mano*," said the tall, lanky boy in a relaxed manner. "Not even a horse could catch it now."

"But we got to," said Juan desperately. "Our families are on that train!"

"Yes," said the tall boy casually, "that's true. But I also have an uncle and aunt back here in León, so I can always catch the next train."

"You mean you still have family back here?" screamed Juan, suddenly getting so raging mad that all fear was gone.

"Well, yes," said the boy, not knowing why Juan was getting so upset.

"Well, then you lied!" screamed Juan. "You tricked me! You didn't make your bet with your whole family on the train!"

The boy only laughed. "Well, no, of course not, *mano*," he said. "Only a fool would bet everything."

"You . . . you . . . !" said Juan.

"Eh, don't swear at me or I'll beat you, Juan. I'm the

strongest boy among us, remember? You wouldn't have a chance."

"I spit on your strength!" said Juan to the bigger, older boy. "I'll fight you to death right now! Come on, let's do it like the devil painted it!"

Seeing Juan's insane rage, the larger boy backed off. "Eh, *mano*, I'm sorry," he said. "Look, you can come and stay with me and my family until we go."

"Stick your family in your pocket!" said Juan. "I'm catching that train!" He picked up his hat and turned, taking off down the tracks.

The train was so far away now that it looked like nothing more than a small dark line, smoking in the distance as it headed for the far end of the long flat valley. Way ahead of the train, Juan could see a bunch of little red-rock hills no bigger than fresh cow-pies, but he didn't lessen his pace. His mother, his most perfect love in all the world, was on that train. So he'd run to the end of the earth if he had to.

〜〜〜
〜〜〜

The sun was high, and Juan talked to God as he went, stepping quickly from tie to tie. He didn't want to wear out the bottoms of his worn-out *huaraches* on the crushed sharp rocks between the wooden ties.

"Oh, dear God," said Juan, watching the tar-painted ties slide under his feet as he went, "I know I've sinned many times in the past, but I swear that I'll never sin again if you help me this time. Give me the wings of an angel so I can fly across this land and catch the train. For remember, you're all-powerful and can do whatever you please and, besides, it's not just me who'll suffer if I die, dear God. It will be my beloved mother who loves you more than life itself!"

And saying this, Juan smiled as he ran on. He liked how he'd added his mother there at the end, and he hoped it would make God feel guilty and force Him to come through and give him the wings of an angel.

But the wings didn't come, so he kept running, eating up the miles. And to his surprise, instead of getting weaker and weaker, he got stronger.

The morning passed by, and Juan noticed that the railroad men had cheated and started putting the ties farther apart. He began to miss the wooden ties as he ran, hitting the sharp rocks instead. Juan's *huaraches* came apart, and twice he had to stop to fix them with a piece of his shirt. He began to get thirsty and thick-tongued, but there were no signs of water anywhere.

"*Ay, Mamá,*" he said, glancing up at the great white sun, "what have I done to us? Without water, even a good man from Los Altos can't survive.

"Oh, dear God," he said, "Lord and master of all the Heavens, forgive me, for I'm a fool. And I know that I played around and gambled when I should have been serious. But . . . well, if you help me this time, dear God, and give me the wings of—look, if it's bothering you to make me an angel because I've never been that good—then how about the wings of an eagle, and I swear that I will never gamble or play around again when I should be serious."

So Juan talked to God, his old companion, who'd helped him all his life. The miles went by and the sun grew hotter and hotter. But not once did he slow down.

He was strong; he'd been raised in the mountains at

nearly six thousand feet, and ever since he could remember, he'd been running from sun to sun with his brother Domingo and their giant cousins, Basilio and Mateo, chasing the wolves and coyotes away from their herds of goats.

But it was hotter down here in the valley. Juan was sweating more than he was used to. The powerful sun grew larger and larger, and the high desert insects began to screech. Once, way ahead in the distance, Juan thought he saw a group of green trees. He figured it had been a water hole.

"Oh, thank you, God," he said, and his mouth began to water, feeling better as he approached the trees.

But then, getting there, he saw that the water hole had long ago dried up. Why, even in the shade of the trees, the earth was nothing but dead-cracked skin.

"Oh, God!" he screamed. "Why do you tease me?"

And he thought he'd die, he was so thirsty. But then he remembered his mother and how she'd lost child after child in the Revolution and he stopped his rage. He had to be strong for her. He glanced around. He saw the little red hills. They were much bigger now. He looked back. The city of León was nothing but a wrinkle in the distance.

"I can make it," he said, taking courage. "I know I can."

He rested a few moments in the shade of the trees along with a few lizards and a fat reddish rattlesnake. Then he took off once again, but this time at an easygoing dog-trot.

The sun, the blanket of the poor, continued its journey across the tall, flat sky, and the day grew so hot that the black tar on the railroad ties melted and came off on his *huaraches*. Heat waves danced in the distance, and mirages of huge blue lakes glistened all around.

Juan became so thirsty that his mouth turned to cotton

and his vision blurred. Finally, he began to walk. He started talking to himself so he wouldn't go crazy. He remembered the stories that his mother had told him of his grandfather, the great Don Pío, and of his two brothers, Cristóbal and Agustín.

Time passed and the insects grew louder and the sun grew hotter, and Juan concentrated way back to those wonderful days up in Los Altos de Jalisco before the Revolution had come to them. He smiled, feeling good, remembering how cool and green the meadows of his youth had been. He smiled and began to trot and thought back to those days of his youth when he and his brother had played with Basilio and Mateo, the two sons of their great uncle Cristóbal.

Oh, those were the days! Playing with those huge, dark Indian-looking men who'd even towered over their father, who was a very big man. Juan ran on. Why, they'd had heavy-boned Indian faces and small yellowish teeth, and they'd been well into the age of wisdom when Juan had first started playing with them. But still, they'd been as simple as children, refusing to live indoors and, instead, had slept under the oak leaves when the weather got cold.

They wouldn't come inside when it rained, but, instead, they loved to race and dance and shout to the heavens every time it stormed. They had no sense of money or personal property and would give away anything that anyone asked of them. They never rode a horse or a burro, but instead, would challenge any horseman to a race across that meadow, over a ridge, and to a distant *barranca*. And they almost always won, even against the fastest horses, because they knew the mountains like the fingers of their hands. And even though many people called them simple, everyone knew that they were not fools.

Oh, he was feeling good now, running up the tracks at a good dog-trot, thinking of his two giant cousins. And no, he would never forget the day that he'd seen his two great cousins follow an armadillo into a cave where they'd found a chest of gold so big that a burro couldn't carry it. Oh, that had been such a wonderful day, taking the mountain of gold home to Don Pío and Uncle Cristóbal.

〰〰〰
〰〰〰

The bottoms of Juan's *huaraches* were gone. The rocks were poking up between them and getting caught in the leather straps. Sitting down on the iron rail, Juan took off his *huaraches* and decided he'd probably be better off barefoot. But walking on the ties, his feet got stuck to the boiling-hot, half-melted tar. He found he was better off going on the sharp stones between the ties.

"Oh, Basilio," he said aloud as he limped along, "if only you and Mateo were here right now to put me on your shoulders and run with me like you used to do when I was a boy." His eyes filled with tears. "But don't worry," he said. "I'm not giving up. Your blood is my blood!"

And saying this, he started loping once again, flying over the stones with his bare feet. He could almost feel his giant cousins here beside him. He'd loved them and they'd loved him, and so they'd always be here inside him, giving him strength, giving wings to his feet. He raced on.

The sun inched its way across the towering flat, blue sky and the little red-rock hills continued dancing between the heat waves in the distance. Juan remembered the day that his brother, Domingo, had finally become so big that he thought he could beat Basilio and Mateo in a foot race.

Boys from all over the mountains came to see. The race was set up in the green meadow by the three lakes.

"But wait," said Basilio. "I don't race for free no more. Every month some new boys want to challenge me and my brother. We got to get paid."

"How much?" said Domingo. He was hot. He really wanted to beat them.

"Well, I don't know," said Basilio, his eyes dancing with merriment. "My brother and I were talking and, well, we figure that we never had enough peanuts to fill our bellies, so we'd like a sack of peanuts."

"Jesus Christ!" screamed Domingo. "That would cost a fortune!"

Basilio and Mateo roared. But Domingo wanted to race, and so he stole one of their father's goats and traded it for a twenty-kilo sack of peanuts.

The marks were set, Domingo and the two giants got in place, and then the call was made and they were off. And Domingo, blue-eyed and red-headed like his father, took off like lightning, barefoot and stripped to the waist. The muscles on his back rippled as his legs and arms worked so fast they became a blur of motion. He was flying, sailing over the short green meadow grass. But he never had a chance. For he'd gone no more than ten yards when the two giants went racing past him, each carrying a young calf on his back like he always did when he raced against human beings and not against horses. They leaped over the short rock fence at the end of the meadow and began to dance with the *gusto* of children.

Oh, those were the days! Domingo had gotten so mad

that his face had become as red as the setting sun. Everyone laughed at him, but he had to admit that he was still a long way from ever beating the giants in a race.

Basilio and Mateo had shared their twenty-kilo sack of peanuts with all of them. They'd had other races between the younger boys and then they'd eat the peanuts—shells and all—so they could fill their starving furnaces of youth.

Juan ran on, feeling tired, drained, exhausted. But he never once lessened his pace. He had his grandfather, Don Pío, in his soul. He had his cousins, Basilio and Mateo, in his legs. And his brothers, Domingo and José, were in his heart. And his mother—the greatest woman in all the world—was waiting for him up ahead. He ran on.

∿
∿

The sun was blasting hot, and the valley was flat and wide and filled with nothing but dead, dry brush. He licked his lips, but found that he had no saliva. So he stopped, picked up a small stone, and wiped it off. He put it in his mouth to suck on. Oh, he'd never forget the day of the race that they'd also bought a basket of oranges and he'd tasted his first orange. They'd cut one into quarters, and he'd seen the luscious slices, juice dripping down, golden and wet and as sweet as honey. He'd eaten three big oranges that day, and he'd felt strong.

Running up the valley, still tasting the sweet-wetness of that golden orange, he now saw that the sun was beginning to slide down the tall, flat sky. Why, he'd run all day without really realizing it. *El ojo de Dios,* the eye of God, was going down and the long, dark shadows of the coming night engulfed him as he came up to the first little hills.

He'd made it across the valley with the help of his family: powerful men and women whose belief in God was so strong that life was indestructible.

He stopped. His feet were swollen and bloody. He wondered if he couldn't find some water here in these little hills and stay for the night before going on.

Looking back, he saw that he must have been climbing for the last hour. The long, flat valley now lay way down below him. There were no traces of León, not even of the smoking burned-out buildings ransacked by revolutionaries.

He turned, going on, and the farther he went, he saw that the hills got taller and the vegetation thicker. Now there were long-shadowed cactus trees and tight, twisted, low-creeping thorny plants. Juan stopped to look for some cactus to suck on. But he was from the mountains, so he didn't know which plant to choose. He sat down to rest. His mouth felt so dry he was choking. But then in his mind's eye he saw his mother, searching for him with her eyes swollen with tears. He struggled to his feet to go on. But his feet hurt so much, he couldn't stand to touch the ground.

"*Ay, Mamá,*" he cried, "please, help me!"

And he continued stumbling up the tracks, with his feet on fire.

Then, coming around a long uphill bend in the tracks, he saw something move ahead of him in the dim light of the going day. Quickly, he grabbed a rock. He figured it was a deer, and so, if he got the chance, he'd hit it on the head and then break its neck so he could suck its blood and eat its meat.

But when he got closer to the rocks where he'd first seen movement, he saw nothing. He glanced all around;

still, he saw nothing but long, dark shadows and the last little thin yellow veins of the evening light.

He was just beginning to believe that it had all been a mistake and he'd seen nothing, when suddenly, there, right before his very eyes—no more than twenty feet away between two small, low rocks—he saw the large round eyes of a jaguar, his spots visible in the dim light.

Juan froze.

"*Ay, Mamá, Mamá,*" he said to himself, losing all courage as he stared at the big cat's eyes. And he wanted to turn and run, but the big cat's tail was now up and moving side to side like an upright snake, hypnotizing him.

The big cat shifted his feet, crouched down, getting ready to leap, and Juan knew this was his last chance to do something. But he was just too scared to move. Then, Juan heard his mother's voice inside him saying, "Attack him, *m'ijito!* Don't run! Attack! Or he'll kill you!"

"*Sí, Mamá,*" he found himself saying. And he let out a howling roar with all his power and attacked the tiger of the desert.

The spotted tiger heard Juan's mighty roar and saw him coming at him in leaping bounds. The big animal leaped up, too, roaring out a terrible scream. But then he turned and ran.

Juan stopped dead in his tracks, turned tail, too, and took off up the side of the tracks as fast as his little legs could go. The big desert cat never looked back. He just kept racing in the other direction.

Juan's feet didn't hurt anymore, and he ran up the tracks without once slowing down until the sun was long gone and the moon came out.

He went all night—walking and running—until he came out of the other side of the small red-rock hills and the morning stars were his companions.

He ran, not stopping, not caring how much his bloody, swollen feet hurt or his throbbing head pained until, way up there in the distance in the darkish daybreak, he thought he saw the little flickering lights of a hundred campfires.

He slowed down, catching his breath, and he could hear people talking. He listened carefully as he came, and then, up ahead in the middle of the flat, he saw the train—the train he'd been after all this time. He began to sob. He'd made it; he'd caught the train. He was going to be able to find his mother and family and not be lost forever and ever.

But then, getting near the campfires, he felt a strange anger come into him. So he circled around the camp—cautious as a coyote, wary as a young deer—making sure that they weren't bandits but were, indeed, his people.

One of the boys who'd raced with him saw him coming.

"*¡Dios mío!*" said the startled boy. "You came the whole way on foot, Juan?"

But Juan couldn't hear the boy, much less see him. Juan was gone. He was as white as a ghost. His whole face and neck and shoulders were white from where the salty sweat had dried on his skin. He was falling, stumbling, gasping, crying as he came toward their fires, white-lipped and wild-eyed.

"Your mother," said the boy, "she said you'd catch us. She told my father last night that you'd . . ."

But Juan paid no attention to the boy. He just walked on, staring at the fires ahead of him. He was hypnotized by the little leaping flames. He was dead on his feet. He'd been running half-conscious since he'd raced away in terror from the spotted desert tiger.

A man turned and saw Juan and leaped up, grabbing him under the armpits just before Juan pitched face-first into the fire.

But, still, Juan's feet kept climbing. He couldn't stop. He had to get past those little dancing hills of flaming fire so he could reach his mother, the love of his life, the only living thing that gave meaning to his entire existence.

Judith Ortiz Cofer

A writer of poetry and prose, Judith Ortiz Cofer was born in Hormigueros, Puerto Rico, in 1952. She grew up on the island as well as in Paterson, New Jersey, and later moved to Atlanta, Georgia, with her family. She earned her B.A. in English from Augusta College, Georgia, in 1974, and an M.A. in English from Florida Atlantic University in 1977. Cofer's work deals with the struggles faced by newer-generation Latinas who have to adopt the modern ways of the Anglo-American culture and flavor it with their own traditional Hispanic origins, forging a new Hispanic-American culture. Among Cofer's works are the collection of essays and poems, *Silent Dancing: A Partial Remembrance of a Puerto Rican Childhood* (1990), and the collection of short stories, *An Island Like You: Stories of the Barrio* (1996). *Silent Dancing*, the author's memoir of her childhood as a Puerto Rican girl living in two cultural realities, earned her the 1991 PEN/Martha Albrand Special Citation for nonfiction and was also named Best Books for the Teen Age by The New York Public Library (1991). *An Island Like You* was awarded the 1995 Pura Belpré Award and named Best Book of the Year (1995–1996) by the American Library Association. Cofer is the co-editor of *Sleeping with One Eye Open: Women Writers and the Art of Survival* (1999). She is the Franklin Professor of English and Creative Writing at the University of Georgia. Her latest novel, *The Meaning of Consuelo* was published in 2003 by Farrar, Strauss and Giroux.

Primary Lessons

My mother walked me to my first day at school at La Escuela Segundo Ruiz Belvis, named after the Puerto Rican patriot born in our town. I remember yellow cement with green trim. All the classrooms had been painted these colors to identify them as government property. This was true all over the Island. Everything was color-coded, including the children, who wore uniforms from first through twelfth grade. We were a midget army in white and brown, led by the hand to our battleground. From practically every house in our barrio emerged a crisply ironed uniform inhabited by the savage creatures we had become over a summer of running wild in the sun.

At my grandmother's house where we were staying until my father returned to Brooklyn Yard in New York and sent for us, it had been complete chaos, with several children to get ready for school. My mother had pulled my hair harder than usual while braiding it, and I had dissolved into a pool of total self-pity. I wanted to stay home with her and Mamá, to continue listening to stories in the late afternoon, to drink *café con leche* with them, and to play rough games with my many cousins. I wanted to continue living the dream of summer afternoons in Puerto Rico, and if I could not have it, then I wanted to go back to Paterson, New Jersey, back to where I imagined our apartment waited, peaceful and cool, for the three of us to return to our former lives. Our gypsy lifestyle had convinced me, at age six, that one part of life

stops and waits for you while you live another for a while—
and if you don't like the present, you can always return to
the past. Buttoning me into my stiff blouse while I tried to
squirm away from her, my mother attempted to explain to
me that I was a big girl now and should try to understand
that, like all the other children my age, I had to go to school.

"What about him?" I yelled, pointing at my brother
who was lounging on the tile floor of our bedroom in his
pajamas, playing quietly with a toy car.

"He's too young to go to school, you know that. Now
stay still." My mother pinned me between her thighs to button my skirt, as she had learned to do from Mamá, from
whose grip it was impossible to escape.

"It's not fair, it's not fair. I can't go to school here. I
don't speak Spanish." It was my final argument, and it failed
miserably because I was shouting my defiance in the language I claimed not to speak. Only I knew what I meant by
saying in Spanish that I did not speak Spanish. I had spent
my early childhood in the U.S., where I lived in a bubble
created by my Puerto Rican parents in a home where two
cultures and languages became one. I learned to listen to the
English from the television with one ear while I heard my
mother and father speaking in Spanish with the other. I
thought I was an ordinary American kid—like the children
on the shows I watched—and that everyone's parents spoke
a secret second language at home. When we came to Puerto Rico right before I started first grade, I switched easily to
Spanish. It was the language of fun, of summertime games.
But school—that was a different matter.

I made one last desperate effort to make my mother see
reason: "Father will be very angry. You know that he wants
us to speak good English." My mother, of course, ignored
me as she dressed my little brother in his playclothes. I

could not believe her indifference to my father's wishes. She was usually so careful about our safety and the many other areas that he was forever reminding her about in his letters. But I was right, and she knew it. Our father spoke to us in English as much as possible, and he corrected my pronunciation constantly—not "jes" but "y-es." Y-es, sir. How could she send me to school to learn Spanish when we would be returning to Paterson in just a few months?

But, of course, what I feared was not language, but loss of freedom. At school there would be no playing, no stories, only lessons. It would not matter if I did not understand a word, and I would not be allowed to make up my own definitions. I would have to learn silence. I would have to keep my wild imagination in check. Feeling locked into my stiffly starched uniform, I only sensed all this. I guess most children can intuit their loss of childhood's freedom on that first day of school. It is separation anxiety, too, but mother is just the guardian of the "playground" of our early childhood.

The sight of my cousins in similar straits comforted me. We were marched down the hill of our barrio where Mamá's robin-egg-blue house stood at the top. I must have glanced back at it with yearning. Mamá's house—a place built for children—where anything that could be broken had already been broken by my grandmother's early batch of offspring (they ranged in age from my mother's oldest sisters to my uncle who was six months older than I was.) Her house had long since been made childproof. It had been a perfect summer place. And now it was September— the cruelest month for a child.

La Mrs., as all the teachers were called, waited for her class of first-graders at the door of the yellow-and-green classroom. She too wore a uniform: it was a blue skirt and a white blouse. This teacher wore black high heels with her "standard issue." I remember this detail because when we were all seated in rows, she called on one little girl and pointed to the back of the room where there were shelves. She told the girl to bring her a shoebox from the bottom shelf. Then, when the box had been placed in her hands, she did something unusual. She had the little girl kneel at her feet and take the pointy high heels off her feet and replace them with a pair of satin slippers from the shoe box. She told the group that every one of us would have a chance to do this if we behaved in her class. Though confused about the prize, I soon felt caught up in the competition to bring *La Mrs.* her slippers in the morning. Children fought over the privilege.

Our first lesson was English. In Puerto Rico, every child has to take twelve years of English to graduate from school. It is the law. In my parents' school days, all subjects were taught in English. The U.S. Department of Education had specified that as a U.S. territory, the Island had to be "Americanized," and to accomplish this task, it was necessary for the Spanish language to be replaced in one generation through the teaching of English in all schools. My father began his school day by saluting the flag of the United States and singing "America" and "The Star-Spangled Banner" by rote, without understanding a word of what he was saying. The logic behind this system was that, though the children did not understand the English words, they would remember the rhythms. Even the games the teacher's manuals required them to play became absurd adaptations. "Here We Go Round the Mulberry Bush" became "Here We Go Round the Mango Tree." I have heard about the confusion caused by the use of a primer in which the sounds of animals were featured. The children were forced to accept that a rooster says *cockadoodledoo,* when they knew perfectly well from hearing their own roosters each morning that in Puerto Rico a rooster says *cocorocó*. Even the vocabulary of their pets was changed; there are still family stories circulating about the bewilderment of a first-grader coming home to try to teach his dog to speak in English. The policy of assimilation by immersion failed on the Island. Teachers adhered to it on paper, substituting their own materials for the texts, but no one took their English home. In due time, the program was minimized to the one class in English per day that I encountered when I took my seat in *La Mrs.*'s first-grade class.

Catching us all by surprise, she stood very straight and tall in front of us and began to sing in English:

"Pollito	Chicken
Gallina	Hen
Lapiz	Pencil
Y Pluma	Pen."

"Repeat after me, children: Pollito—chicken," she commanded in her heavily accented English that only I understood, being the only child in the room who had ever been exposed to the language. But I too remained silent. No use making waves, or showing off. Patiently *La Mrs.* sang her song and gestured for us to join in. At some point it must have dawned on the class that this silly routine was likely to go on all day if we did not "repeat after her." It was not her fault that she had to follow the rule in her teacher's manual stating that she must teach English *in* English, and that she must not translate, but merely repeat her lesson in English until the children "begin to respond" more or less "unconsciously." This was one of the vestiges of the regimen followed by her predecessors in the last generation. To this day I can recite "Pollito—Chicken" mindlessly, never once pausing to visualize chicks, hens, pencils, or pens.

I soon found myself crowned "teacher's pet" without much effort on my part. I was a privileged child in her eyes simply because I lived in "Nueva York," and because my father was in the navy. His name was an old one in our pueblo, associated with once-upon-a-time landed people and long-gone money. Status is judged by unique standards in a culture where, by definition, everyone is a second-class citizen. Remembrance of past glory is as good as titles and money. Old families living in decrepit old houses rank over factory workers living in modern comfort in cement boxes—all the same. The professions raise a person out of the dreaded "sameness" into a niche of status, so that teachers, nurses, and everyone who went to school for a job were given the honorifics of *El Míster* or *La Mrs.* by the common folks, people who were likely to be making more money in American factories than the poorly paid educators and government workers.

My first impressions of the hierarchy began with my teacher's shoe-changing ceremony and the exaggerated respect she received from our parents. *La Mrs.* was always right, and adults scrambled to meet her requirements. She wanted all our school books covered in the brown paper now used for paper bags (used at that time by the grocer to wrap meats and other foods). That first week of school the grocer was swamped with requests for paper, which he gave away to the women. That week and the next, he wrapped produce in newspapers. All school projects became family projects. It was considered disrespectful at Mamá's house to do homework in privacy. Between the hours when we came home from school and dinner time, the table was shared by all of us working together with the women hovering in the background. The teachers communicated directly with the mothers, and it was a matriarchy of far-reaching power and influence.

There was a black boy in my first-grade classroom who was also the teacher's pet but for a different reason than I: I did not have to do anything to win her favor; he would do anything to win a smile. He was as black as the cauldron that Mamá used for cooking stew, and his hair was curled into tight little balls on his head—*pasitas,* like little raisins glued to his skull, my mother had said. There had been some talk at Mamá's house about this boy; Lorenzo was his name. I later gathered that he was the grandson of my father's nanny. Lorenzo lived with Teresa, his grandmother, having been left in her care when his mother took off for "Los Nueva Yores" shortly after his birth. And they were poor. Everyone could see that his pants were too big for him—hand-me-downs—and his shoe soles were as thin as paper. Lorenzo seemed unmindful of the giggles he caused when he jumped up to erase the board for *La Mrs.* and his baggy pants rode down to his thin hips as he strained up to get every stray mark. He seemed to relish playing the little clown when she asked him to come to the front of the room and sing his phonetic version of "obootifool, forpashios-keeis" leading the class in our incomprehensible tribute to the American flag. He was a bright, loving child, with a talent for song and mimicry that everyone commented on. He should have been chosen to host the PTA show that year instead of me.

At recess one day, I came back to the empty classroom to get something. My cup? My nickel for a drink from the kioskman? I don't remember. But I remember the conversation my teacher was having with another teacher. I remember because it concerned me, and because I memorized it so that I could ask my mother to explain what it meant.

"He is a funny *negrito,* and, like a parrot, he can repeat anything you teach him. But his Mamá must not have the money to buy him a suit."

"I kept Rafaelito's First Communion suit; I bet Lorenzo could fit in it. It's white with a bow-tie," the other teacher said.

"But, Marisa," laughed my teacher, "in that suit, Lorenzo would look like a fly drowned in a glass of milk."

Both women laughed. They had not seen me crouched at the back of the room, digging into my schoolbag. My name came up then.

"What about the Ortiz girl? They have money."

"I'll talk to her mother today. The superintendent, *El Americano* from San Juan, is coming down for the show. How about if we have her say her lines in both Spanish and English?"

The conversation ends there for me. My mother took me to Mayagüez and bought me a frilly pink dress and two crinoline petticoats to wear underneath so that I looked like a pink-and-white parachute with toothpick legs sticking out. I learned my lines, "Padres, maestros, Mr. Leonard, bienvenidos/Parents, teachers, Mr. Leonard, welcome . . ." My first public appearance. I took no pleasure in it. The words were formal and empty. I had simply memorized them. My dress pinched me at the neck and arms, and made me itch all over.

I had asked my mother what it meant to be a "mosca en un vaso de leche," a fly in a glass of milk. She had laughed at the image, explaining that it meant being "different," but that it wasn't something I needed to worry about.

Volar

At twelve I was an avid consumer of comic books—*Super-girl* was my favorite. I spent my allowance of a quarter a day on two twelve-cent comic books or a double issue for twenty-five. In my bedroom closet I had a stack of *Legion of Super Heroes* and *Supergirl* comic books that was as tall as I.

I had a recurring dream in those days: that I had long blonde hair and could fly. In my dream I climbed the stairs to the top of our apartment building as myself, but as I went up each flight, changes would be taking place. Step by step I would fill out: my legs would grow long, my arms harden into steel, and my hair would magically go straight and turn a golden color. Of course, I would add the bonus of breasts, but not too large; Supergirl had to be aerodynamic, and sleek and hard as a supersonic missile. Once on the roof, my parents safely asleep in their beds, I would get on tiptoe, arms outstretched in the position for flight, and jump out of my fifth-story-high window into the black lake of the sky. From up there, over the rooftops, I could see everything, even beyond the few blocks of our barrio; with my X-ray vision I could look inside the homes of people who interested me.

Once I saw our landlord, whom I knew my parents feared, sitting in a treasure-room dressed in an ermine coat and a large gold crown. He sat on the floor counting his dollar bills. I played a trick on him. Going up to his building's chimney, I blew a little puff of my super-breath into his fireplace, scattering his stacks of money so that he had to start counting all over again.

I could more or less program my Supergirl dreams in those days by focusing on the object of my current obsession. This way I saw into the private lives of my neighbors, my teachers, and in the last days of my childish fantasy and the beginning of adolescence, into the secret rooms of the boys I liked. In the mornings I'd wake up in my tiny bedroom with its incongruous—at least in our tiny apartment—white "princess" furniture my mother had chosen for me, and find myself back in my body—my tight curls still clinging to my head, my skinny arms and legs and flat chest unchanged.

In the kitchen my mother and father would be talking softly over a *café con leche*. She would come "wake me" exactly forty-five minutes after they had gotten up. It was their time together at the beginning of each day, and even at an early age I could feel their disappointment if I interrupted them by getting up too early. So I would stay in my bed recalling my dreams of flight, perhaps planning my next flight. In the kitchen they would be discussing events in the barrio. Actually, my father would be carrying that part of the conversation; when it was her turn to speak, she would, more often than not, try shifting the topic toward her desire to see her *familia* on the Island: How about a vacation in Puerto Rico together this year, *querido?* We could rent a car, go to the beach. We could . . . And he would answer patiently, gently: *Mi amor,* do you know how much it would cost for all of us to fly there? It is not possible for me to take the time off . . . *Mi vida,* please understand . . . And I knew that soon she would rise from the table. Not abruptly. She would light a cigarette and look out the kitchen window. The view was of a dismal alley that was littered with refuse thrown from windows. The space was too narrow for anyone larger than a skinny child to enter safely, so it was never cleaned. My mother would check the time on the clock over her sink, the one with a prayer for patience and grace written in Spanish. A birthday gift. She would see that it was time to wake me. She'd sigh deeply and say the same thing the view from her kitchen window always inspired her to say: "*Ay, si yo pudiera volar.*"

Additional Works by These Authors

Chacón, Daniel. *Chicano, Chicanery*. Houston, Arte Público Press, 2000.

Colón, Jesús. *Lo que el pueblo me dice...* Houston, Arte Público Press, 2001.

_____. *The Way It Was and Other Writings*. Houston, Arte Público Press, 1993.

de la Garza, Beatriz. *The Candy Vendor's Boy and Other Stories*. Houston, Arte Público Press, 1994.

_____. *Pillars of Gold and Silver*. Houston, Arte Público Press, 1997.

Esteves, Sandra María. *Bluestown Mockingbird Mambo*. Houston, Arte Público Press, 1990.

Fernández, Roberta. *Fronterizas: Una novela en seis cuentos*. Houston, Arte Público Press, 2001.

_____. *Intaglio: A Novel in Six Stories*. Houston, Arte Público Press, 1990.

Martí, José. *Versos Sencillos / Simple Verses*. Manuel A. Tellechea, trans. Houston, Arte Público Press, 1997.

Mora, Pat. *The Bakery Lady / La señora de la panadería*. Houston, Arte Público Press, 2001.

_____. *Borders*. Houston, Arte Público Press, 1996.

_____. *Chants*. Houston, Arte Público Press, 1994.

_____. *Communion*. Houston, Arte Público Press, 1991.

_____. *Delicious Hullabaloo / Pachanga deliciosa*. Houston, Arte Público Press, 1995.

_____. *The Desert Is My Mother / El desierto es mi madre*. Houston, Arte Público Press, 1994.

_____. *The Gift of the Poinsettia / El regalo de la flor de

Nochebuena. Houston, Arte Público Press, 1995.

_____. *My Own True Name: New and Selected Poems for Young Adults, 1984–1999.* Houston, Arte Público Press, 2000.

Ortiz Cofer, Judith. *Bailando en silencio: Escenas de una niñez puertorriqueña.* Houston, Arte Público Press, 1997.

_____. *Silent Dancing: A Partial Remembrance of a Puerto Rican Childhood.* Houston, Arte Público Press, 1991.

_____. *Terms of Survival.* Houston, Arte Público Press, 1995.

_____. *The Year of Our Revolution.* Houston, Arte Público Press, 1998.

Padilla, Mike. *Hard Language.* Houston, Arte Público Press, 2000.

Rivera, Tomas. *The Searchers: Collected Poetry.* Houston, Arte Público Press, 1990.

_____. *Tomás Rivera: The Complete Works.* Houston, Arte Público Press, 1995.

_____. *...y no se lo tragó la tierra / ...And the Earth Did Not Devour Him.* Evangelina Vigil-Piñón, trans. Houston, Arte Público Press, 1995.

Suárez, Virgil. *The Cutter.* Houston, Arte Público Press, 1998.

_____. *Infinite Refuge.* Houston, Arte Público Press, 1995.

_____. *Spared Angola: Memories from a Cuban-American Childhood.* Houston, Arte Público Press, 2002.

Treviño, Jesús Salvador. *The Fabulous Sinkhole and Other Stories.* Houston, Arte Público Press, 1995.

Villaseñor, Victor. *Walking Stars.* Houston, Arte Público Press, 2003.

Viramontes, Helena María. *The Moths and Other Stories.* Houston, Arte Público Press, 1995.